Endorsements

"I spent approximately 20 years working as a church consultant. During this time, my efforts were focused on training church leaders to function as equippers. Among all the pastors and leaders, I had the privilege of relating to, Charlie Halley proved to be an "All Star." I watched him relate to those he led in a way that enabled them to soar in their respective roles. When it came to equipping others for Kingdom service, Charlie simply "got it." He now writes a book forged in real life experience and I highly recommend it to anyone who wants to lead as Jesus did."

Don Cousins
Lead Pastor, Discovery Church (Orlando)

"Having walked with Charlie for years, I can confidently say that what you will read in this book not only oozes from every pore of his body, but works in the life of a church. As one who is naturally intuitive and impatient for results, I can attest that systematically ingesting these truths and living them out helped me become a better leader and launched our church into place of fruitfulness that I had not experienced corporately in 25 years of ministry. I highly recommend this read for anyone who is serious about the church being a place where Jesus would call home."

Sean Richmond
Overseer, Antioch New England

Programs are easy. Values are hard. The House of Jesus is taking the right road to building a local church or missional community to living out the values of Jesus. Programs can start at the grass roots and work up. Values start at the top and work their way through the entire organization. Jesus is the Head of the Church and His values are to permeate the entire body of Christ...in its thinking, motivations, and actions.

Every pastor, staff, and board member needs to read Charlie Halley's book to pray, and commit to building the House of Jesus, His way!

Bruce Bugbee
Bruce Bugbee and Associates

"I have always loved Charlie Halley. Reading his latest book made my admiration for him grow even more. This book truly reveals the Charlie I know—a man zealous to help the Church operate in a manner worthy to be called the House of Jesus."

Branson Sheets
Lead Pastor, Covenant Church (Greenville, NC)

"Charlie Halley has found a narrative that is much needed within the body of Christ. The balance of personal learnings and real-life stories found a way to connect me to a challenging truth; our church culture must be aligned to the leadership of Christ. This book finds a way to challenge us not only in what must be done, but in how to do it. Filled with tools and additional resources, "The House of Jesus" will change how we equip and live out Jesus' mission for us. Reading this book taught me, but more importantly challenged me and gave me the resources to act."

Brian Zehr
Founder, Intentional Impact

I highly recommend 'The House of Jesus' as a powerful resource for anyone seeking to rediscover the beauty of a healthy church. I've witnessed firsthand, in a variety of different situations, the power of these insights at work in local congregations as we learn how to align to Jesus.

Drew Steadman
US Director, Antioch Movement (Waco, TX)

"Charlie's simple frameworks presented in this book provide an excellent guide for leaders to use as they invest in others and I should know. I have personally benefited from Charlie's mentorship and am eternally thankful for his paradigm shifting investment in me as a leader.

As the overseer of Engage the Crisis (a project where 2,000 volunteers were sent to serve during the European refugee crisis), I leveraged Charlie's tools to guide our leaders for how to identify giftings on their teams, apprentice team members into needed roles, and coach them into effectiveness. The project was greatly aided by his innovation."

Chris McBride
Task Force Director, 24:14 Coalition

Charlie's commitment to the church and passion for a community based in grace and empowering leadership is inspiring. I appreciate the attention to detail to unpack the church as a home that is congruent with its designer and chief cornerstone.

Justin Dorroh
Director, Antioch Discipleship School

"I have known Charlie Halley in the context of a consultant, a mentor, a co-worker and a caring friend. In all these settings, his driving passion remains the same: to emulate God's way of doing ministry and then equip others to do the same. Charlie and his insights in "The House of Jesus" will greatly benefit all those who are eager to learn how to equip the saints for the work of ministry. With fresh and timely perspective, this book profoundly answers the question -- "how does God do ministry?" -- in a deeply biblical yet highly practical way that will be useful for all who read."

John Prickett
Director of Ministry, Antioch Community Church (Boston)

To every one of my apprentices;

past, present and future.

May this work enable you to catalyze

Kingdom culture more than I ever could.

THE HOUSE OF JESUS

WHERE LOVE AND EQUIPPING
FUEL HIS MESSAGE

Charles Halley

Contents

Acknowledgements

There are countless sets of fingerprints within this book.

I have strived to make the Father's, Jesus' and the Holy Spirit's the primary ones, but many of Their followers have influenced me over the decades.

I am grateful to numerous Kingdom champions in my life: Don Cousins, Bruce Bugbee, Bob Tuttle, Bill Pannell, George Ladd, David Smith, Bill Easum, Danny Silk, Blake Hartsock, Brian Zehr and Rick Bewsher to name just a few. Each spoke life-altering, Gospel truth into me.

I am obviously grateful for amazing partners in ministry over the years: Bob Walkup, David Brownlee, Branson Sheets, Sean Richmond and Mark Buckner stand out among many. Thank you for your trust as I walked out my gifting.

My apprentices have taught me more than they realize. Darlynn Sakowski, Melissa Norris, John Prickett, Brian Marchioni, Neil Hubacker, Micah Scharchburg and many others are excelling beyond me! Amen!

If you look closely in this work, you can also find the contributions of many of my Kingdom friends like John Halley, Neil Hubacker, John Prickett, Trinity Robb, Bill Edwards, Tom and Judy Skaff, David Gladney, Chris McBride, Justin Dorroh, Micah Scharchburg,

Rod Vestal, Bruce Mazzare, Jeff and Tania Palen. Your observations, feedback and tough questions propelled me forward! A grateful shout out to my editor, Jenny Tak. You were a game-changer. Trust me, her contributions are on every page!

And last, but not least, are the fingerprints of my wife, Mary Lou. She has been my most faithful friend, intercessor and cheerleader over the years. Without her patient and encouraging words as I wrote and rewrote, I probably would have given up.

Chapter One

Searching for Jesus' House

John, Lynn and Sam gave their lives to Jesus on the same day and when they did, everything changed.

All three were students at the same school and because of this shared experience, a deep bond was forged between them that would last for years. During these early months of walking with Jesus, they frequently got together to share what they were learning. There were lots of things to talk about.

From the very beginning, each was deeply stirred as they heard Jesus through His "still, small voice" and the four Gospels. Following their new Lord and Savior seemed to catalyze multiple places of breakthrough every day. All were thrilled to begin experiencing freedom in areas of their lives where longstanding lies had taken them prisoner.

John, Lynn and Sam were awed by all that they were learning and experiencing. As they continued to share life together, their conversations kept coming back to three foundational truths about Jesus.

Each was learning about the immeasurable depth and breadth of Jesus. An all sufficient Lord who is worthy of worship. A Teacher whose redemptive message was unlike anything they had ever heard. Jesus' claims of deity became more believable every day.

Not to mention that Jesus was also a master communicator; He used just the right words at just the right time. And not only was Jesus His Father's anointed spokesperson, He was a Friend with whom each could share their daily life.

They were also learning about Jesus' never-ending capacity to genuinely love them and all peoples of the world. Their Savior was authentic and gentle and patient and so many other facets of love. Even when others plotted Jesus' demise or betrayed Him, He did not return evil with evil, but extended grace and forgiveness. Each of them craved a community where they could live life among Jesus-like people where each could be themselves and feel safe. They were tasting it during this season and wanted more.

Finally, they were discovering what a great leader Jesus was. As they learned and processed how He influenced others, they were deeply impressed. The three had had multiple bosses and agreed that none of them were like Jesus. He possessed so much clarity about His mission and was more than patient as He equipped and empowered His follower's God-given capacities. Each was wowed by how Jesus always invested more into His disciples than He asked from them; how novel compared to the world they had grown up in.

As this learning process unfolded, they also started to encounter Jesus in one another and in the community of disciples all three had joined. For the first time, they felt the presence of God in a larger context – the power of Jesus' message together with lifegiving worship. The unconditional acceptance and encouraging words they received from older believers were an unexpected blessing. What a counter-cultural experience: a community of loving relationships in contrast to the selfish network of friends each of them had grown up with. Last but not least, they were more than surprised to find themselves being empowered to help lead. All three were excited to jump into ministry to a nearby neighborhood.

Their shared experience within this house of Jesus marked each of them deeply. The combination of Jesus' message, selfless love and equipping-based empowerment had catalyzed the power of God's Spirit in and around them in ways that were beyond words.

As John, Lynn and Sam approached graduation, they met together one last time. Together, they recounted the amazing journey they had had with one another and with Jesus; what a ride! As they said their goodbyes, they made a heartfelt covenant with one another: *Wherever God leads, each of us will find an established house of Jesus; a gathering of followers where Jesus' life-giving message is fueled by His selfless love and equipping-based empowerment.*

As they went their separate ways, they assumed that it would be relatively easy to find Jesus houses that would be like Him, but that was not their experience.

John's path led to graduate studies in accounting and a related calling to avocational ministry in the marketplace. As his life unfolded, he kept walking with Jesus and made a real effort to find a Jesus house in keeping with the covenant he had made. John visited numerous churches and kept finding the same problems. In each place, the preaching content sounded like the Master and the life principles shared were spiritually relevant, but significant elements were always missing. These Jesus houses consistently lacked His relational values and warmth. And more often than not, they seemed to value centralized power and control more than His equipping-based empowerment. John appreciated his time in these *Jesus' Message houses*, but kept looking for one that was more like Him. His discouragement became debilitating; never quite finding what he had experienced with Lynn and Sam.

After graduation, Lynn pursued an international vision she had had for years. Her studies had focused on global marketing and like John, she felt called to share Jesus through her marketplace career. In time, she was thrilled to accept a new job, move to an international hub and launch her dream.

The first Jesus house she visited in this country made a positive first impression. She quickly connected with its participants and was very encouraged initially. But within a few weeks, Lynn realized that the message of the Master was missing. His truths were almost nowhere to be found and instead, replaced with a mixture of cultural jargon, personal stories and human wisdom. Lynn's heart was warmed by these relationships, but the absence of Jesus' redemptive Gospel was both shocking and frustrating. She also noticed that this church's leadership quickly empowered its people, but not like Jesus; there was little to no equipping. Lynn knew she needed to keep looking for an authentic Jesus house that was more like Him, but all she found were Jesus' Love houses. And like John, she grew increasingly discouraged. She was not finding any Jesus houses intentionally aligned to His life-giving message, selfless love and equipping-based empowerment.

Sam's journey after graduation was very different than John and Lynn's. He had completed a degree in psychology, but had never had their clarity of purpose and direction. Without any clear calling, he starting working in short-term jobs while he continued to prayerfully seek God's guidance. In time, Sam discovered the Father's best through the eyes of others and a confirmation from God's Spirit: a calling to full-time, vocational ministry.

After an extended season of preparation, Sam received an invitation to serve a Jesus house as one of its pastors. It had been a lengthy discernment process, but Sam was fully confident that he had found a Jesus house that was committed to saying what He said and living like He lived.

As Sam began his ministry, it did not take long for him to affirm that this Jesus house was a spiritually vibrant community. He so appreciated its commitment to preaching Jesus' Gospel with passion and clarity. He could see the impact the house had made and was making in their city.

He was also encouraged by the humility, authenticity and generosity within this community. House leaders had been working diligently to prioritize loving relationships in spite of numerous cultural challenges. The percentage of broken families in Sam's new city was staggering. So he was greatly encouraged that leadership had launched a holistic outreach to address these significant needs; lives were being changed.

But later that same year, John began getting in touch with his growing frustrations with the house's leadership culture; a sharp contrast to Jesus' equipping-based empowerment. He liked and respected many of the leaders and had initially been so encouraged to find this *Jesus' Message and Love house*. But all of its good qualities were being drowned out by wave after wave of leadership dysfunction. As an insider, he now had a front row seat to see the leadership's values, norms and behaviors: power plays, people being used, sexism, manipulation, micro-managing and more. Given the sales pitch he had heard before joining the staff, this reality was a stunning and devastating discovery. Now what?

John, Lynn and Sam stayed in touch through these life transitions, though nothing like what they had enjoyed in school. Unexpectedly, they met up at a friend's wedding almost exactly 5-years after meeting Jesus. They were thrilled to see each other again and have some time to catch up, and that is what they did. Late into the night, they shared story after story about their life with Jesus, His houses and what they had been learning.

Simultaneously together, they encountered a moment of Holy Spirit revelation:

Every Jesus house they had visited these past five years had a common flaw. Each had unknowingly imported one or more values from the surrounding culture, rather than be fully aligned to Him.

How obvious in retrospect!

Every geographical context they had lived in is marked by deep-seated, worldly values, voices and behaviors that are at war with Jesus' message and culture—arrogance, pride, racism, abuse, control, selfishness, sexism, greed, pragmatism etc. To be sure, some settings are more difficult than others, but every imperfect human brings the world's toxins with them into Jesus' house.

After the wedding, they once again said their goodbye's, but Sam just couldn't stop thinking about their collective stories, experiences and "a-ha" moment. All the way home, he kept meditating on several relevant Bible passages: *"For My thoughts are not your thoughts and your ways are not My ways."*[1] *"See to it that no one takes you captive through hollow and deceptive philosophy, which depends on human tradition and the elemental spiritual forces of this world rather than Christ."*[2] Sam was desperate for clarity and answers.

The first morning home, Sam opened the Bible and a journal and invited the Godhead – Father, Son and Holy Spirit – to show him the way. For days, he scribed all that he was learning about Jesus' house and on one, ordinary morning, another light bulb went on. Finally, the pieces of the puzzle were starting to fall into place and he started typing an e-mail to John and Lynn entitled *Today's Convictions:*

Dear friends,

So great to see you both last month! Since we met up, I haven't stopped processing all that we discussed and the insights we had together.

As able, I'd love your input on my new insights below.

Love you both, Sam

A faithful house of Jesus keeps striving to ...

---

[1] Is 55:8-9
[2] Col 2:8-9

#1: *Make Jesus the Cornerstone to which everything is aligned*

#2: *Say what He Said (An incarnational testimony of God's grace)*

#3: *Be who He Was (A selfless love for others)*

#4: *Do what He Did (A passion for equipping-based empowerment)*

Jesus is honored by John, Lynn and Sam's desire to align their lives to His thoughts and ways.

Jesus lived in their world and is well aware of its brokenness.

Jesus is all too familiar with conflicted "houses" like the ones they have experienced and knows that these communities cannot prevail (Mt 6:24).

After the Spirit's arrival on Pentecost, the leaders Jesus had mentored followed His example, and a catalytic move of God was launched (Acts 1-2; 4:11). These are the kinds of Jesus houses that John, Lynn and Sam have been looking for!

Unfortunately, worldly values, norms and behaviors have neutered the house of Jesus for centuries.

I also relate easily to these three friends, especially Sam.

I have worshiped in and served Jesus houses like the ones they have experienced. These challenges have fueled my relentless pursuit to understand what it means for Jesus to be a house's cornerstone.

Jesus has taught me in depth about the power of clarity and how to accelerate a community's alignment to His relational and equipping values.

I have led conflicted communities to places of greater unity, faithfulness and effectiveness. None became perfect; all became more aligned to Jesus' words and ways.

I have mentored hungry leaders like John, Lynn and Sam for more than twenty years.

I have pondered and researched Jesus' culture of selfless love and equipping-based empowerment for decades. I wrote on this subject awhile back and am doing so again in hopes of providing better resources for communities choosing to plant and accelerate Jesus' houses.

I will be utilizing **HouseofJesus.net** as a platform to provide individuals, teams and communities with multiple paths for ongoing learning on this book's themes.

Windows into My Perceptions

Here are a handful of stories from my own life that echo the experiences of John, Lynn and Sam:

Beginnings

I was naïve when I first started vocational ministry.

I had recently completed a multi-year training process to be a pastor that included an internship. This intentional preparation had given me a measure of confidence in my God-given capacity to help people understand and experience His grace. Along the way, I had also been apprenticed in how best to communicate with people and build teams. The result: my vision for serving students in my new, Midwestern hometown was pretty clear and I had a general strategy for how to get there. But what I did not yet understand— nor did I even have a grid for—was the clash between God's values and His enemy's within the local church.

This first pastoral role was located in a region dominated by large-scale manufacturing. The vast majority of people living in the area were employed by an industrial giant or one of its suppliers.

For many years, this company had created a work culture of control, distrust and manipulation. Predictably, I continually ran into obstacles as I began to define and build Kingdom culture within my ministry area. My Gospel ideals kept getting blocked by long-standing, worldly behaviors that had taken root within the house of God I served.

What an eye-opening season that was for me. For the first time, I had a front row seat to witness how the values of the surrounding culture can infect the body of Christ. But I also learned about the power of God's Spirit and His ways in that same setting. My leadership team persistently affirmed and modeled a new culture of Christ within our student ministry that broke ranks with the past. Honor, authenticity and empowerment gradually became the new reality and set the stage for a vibrant ministry.

Serving in the midst of this congregational duplicity was hard, but the lessons I learned through it have never ceased to inform my ministry leadership.

Andy's Story

Nothing prepared my friend for what transpired after he was hired to serve as a Lead Pastor for the first time.

From the outset of the interview process, Andy and his wife were encouraged by their time with church leaders. The search committee seemed so clear in their hopes for the future and easily articulated desired outcomes for their leader. Ultimately, the committee came to the same conclusion my friends did: this church home and Andy were a great fit.

Once Andy began his new role, the initial months reinforced his first positive impressions. Toward the end of the first year, however, reality of the community's disunity reared its ugly head. It became increasingly clear that Andy was serving a divided house with two, competing factions.

The trigger for this open conflict was his work with church leaders and congregants to affirm written statements detailing the community's vision, mission and values. I had been coaching Andy and his team through each step. Unfortunately, my upfront warning was spot on: The process of clarifying vision and values sometimes exposes disunity.

Long story short, this initiative had revealed a sizeable portion of the congregation who did not affirm the Great Commission as the defining purpose of the church. How painful it was for Andy and his wife to discover that a fierce battle between the values of consumerism and God's priority for reaching the lost was taking place inside the congregation. And it was even more painful and challenging when many within this faction left in a huff.

After several grueling years, a unified, Jesus-aligned culture emerged within that household that in turn set the stage for an effective ministry that transformed lives. Andy and I both learned a lot through this process.

David's Challenge

As soon as my friend David challenged me, I knew God was calling me to go.

In my mid-forties, I sensed that it was God's plan for me to write a book and capture what I had been learning for the past twenty-plus years. Staff leadership positions in multiple churches, heading up a business turnaround, graduate degrees in theology and business, plus external consulting experiences with a number of churches had resulted in a handful of strong convictions about the power of a clear Kingdom culture.

Throughout the writing process, I kept getting good feedback from David. Shortly after a full draft was completed, he called me and asked if I could meet him at a local coffee shop. I always enjoyed our conversations, but this huddle ended up being quite a surprise.

David cut to the chase quickly and shared that he was moving to a nearby city to be the Lead Pastor of a large congregation that was fracturing. Having detailed his mission to reestablish a God-honoring culture, he popped the question: "Charlie, would you be my Executive Pastor and partner with me in this journey?" Almost immediately I said, "Thanks but no thanks," but his retort rocked me spiritually. "Now that you have written a book on Kingdom-based strategies that renews the house of God, you need to walk the talk in order to validate them. Here's your opportunity!"

Seven months later, our family moved to engage this crisis that became an eight-year mission.

This season in my life confirmed both my book's premise and my life experiences to date: a Christian community whose identity is persistently aligned to Jesus' grace and values catalyzes godly unity and sets the stage for the Spirit's renewal.Day after day, week after week, month after month, we kept pounding Jesus' core values deeper into the community's culture and tried our best to collectively walk them out. This life experience confirmed like never before that God accomplishes immeasurably more than all we ask or imagine.

New England

Sean and the first pioneers arrived in New England in 1998 to launch a church planting movement. Fifteen years later, he and the Elders graciously invited me to jump in as a leader. The goal of their open door was to add a missing gift-mix to the lead team as well as a seasoned perspective in ministry. This new opportunity was everything I had expected and more: challenging, invigorating, heart-stretching and deep learning experience.

As I partnered with Sean, we were constantly learning from one another as "iron sharpens iron" and that reality continues to this day. As it relates to Kingdom culture, listen as Sean describes several insights he gained from our many discussions on godly leadership.

"Intuition is a common leadership quality within our movement and my circle of church planting friends. It's hard for me to even imagine not having this capacity that includes easily seeing the big picture and future possibilities. This "six sense" has also been invaluable in picking up the heart cues of those I serve every day. At the same time, it has also created its own leadership challenges which in turn, has triggered multiple learnings.

First, I now understand more fully that the vast majority of people are not as intuitive as me. That's not a bad thing; I benefit tremendously from my friends and co-workers who are wired to be detail oriented and practical. Where would I be without them!

But I have also learned that most of these people cannot easily decode my intuition. Too often in the past, I have assumed that my staff, leaders and church family fully understood my core values for ministry when in fact, they did not.

More than ever, I appreciate the frustration my lack of clarity created and am very committed to codifying Jesus' ways. In fact, Kingdom culture and what that means and looks like has never been clearer within our Boston-based movement. I am seeing signs of increased harvest as a result. Thank you, Lord!"

Tom and Judy's Story

My friends Tom and Judy spent their fifties serving Jesus in several Asian countries. Recently, they returned to one of them to be training facilitators for a week in a Northern region they had never visited before.

Their goal was straightforward: to provide new and seasoned pastors with a basic, biblical template for serving their communities. All in all, it was a fruitful week of ministry and participants were very grateful for Tom and Judy's leadership. But my friends witnessed one very interesting cultural obstacle as Judy later described.

"Charlie, on the third day of our training, one of the more seasoned pastors present had an amazing breakthrough. His story really underscores the need for the stated Kingdom values you champion.

It was clear to us that this pastor's understanding of God's saving grace was rock solid and firmly grounded in the Bible. In fact, this was one of his greatest strengths. But at the same time, it was also obvious that his leadership style mimicked the culture of indigenous religions in this country combined with a sprinkle of 19th century Western missionaries. Bottom line: He expected his faith community to revere him and approach him as though he was a guru.

The focal point of our teaching that morning was Philippians 2; a powerful picture of Jesus' humility and sacrificial service to mankind. As the group processed these verses and mined its implications, he was shaken to the core. In the hours that followed, his whole philosophy of pastoral leadership changed. His self-centric attitude which had been undermining his ministry gave way to selfless humility.

It was a beautiful transformation that once again highlighted that wherever you serve God's house on this globe, the cultures of our world always war against Kingdom values."

Aligning a House to Jesus

Like Sam, I've been writing down what I have been learning. And if I were sharing a quick summary with you over coffee, here are the four, foundational steps to begin aligning any house to Jesus.

#1: Make Jesus the House's Cornerstone

Peter and Paul agree with Jesus that He is the definition of plumb for His houses. This process will include steps like:

- House leaders collectively affirming and maintaining the supremacy of Jesus' words and ways;
- An ongoing discipline of training that enables leaders to understand and articulate what it means for Jesus to be the cornerstone of a house;
- A relentless passion among leaders to root out any worldly values that are hindering Jesus' house.

#2: Incarnationally Testify to God's Grace

Say what He said!
The "manifold wisdom of God" is that through Jesus, we can approach the Father with freedom and confidence (Eph 3:10-12). This process will include steps like:

- Leaders modeling daily intimacy with Jesus;
- Worship that honors the Father's extravagant grace;
- Contextualizing Jesus' message through being His hands and ambassadors;
- Apprenticing disciples in spiritual warfare.

#3: Catalyze a Jesus-Aligned, Relational Culture

Be who He was!
Love is primary for the Father and Jesus, and so it always leads the way. This process will include steps like:
- Persistent intercession for godly relationships and unity;
- Teaching and modeling what loving relationships look like;
- Establishing transferable cornerstone values for selfless relationships;
- Embracing ongoing alignment to these values and related heart discipleship.

#4: Catalyze a Jesus-Aligned, Equipping Culture

Do what He did!
The Father and Jesus equip and empower faithful disciples for opportunities to serve that have been prepared in advance (Eph 2:10). This process will include steps like:
- Persistent intercession for God to send workers into His harvest field;
- Teaching and modeling what it looks like to walk in our God-honoring anointing;
- Establishing cornerstone values for godly equipping-based empowerment;
- Embracing ongoing alignment to these values and related ministry discipleship;
- Forming a decentralized leadership community among all leaders and their apprentices.

The House of Jesus is primarily focused on these last two points: *How can a disciple catalyze a Jesus-aligned culture of relationships and equipping that fuels His Gospel of grace?*

Lord, help us to follow Your example!

THE HOUSE OF JESUS

Chapter Two

Cornerformity

Consequently, you are no longer foreigners and strangers, but fellow citizens with God's people and also members of His household, built on the foundation of the apostles and prophets, with Christ Jesus himself as the chief cornerstone

EPH 2:19-20

Virtually every adult understands the implications of living in someone else's home.

First and foremost, living in another person's home means that they are the ones in charge, not you. Secondly, it is their sole right to establish the home's culture – its defining values, behaviors and norms. Once in place, these boundaries inform any resident on what is important, how they should behave, and what community contributions are expected.

The Old Testament affirms that these same earthly realities also apply to God's domain. The "house of God" is just that: it is a community where *I AM*[1] is honored and worshipped. And as expected, the Father's values and norms guide His house's inhabitants. Specifically, all people are to be treated justly and with mercy. Additionally, residents of God's house are expected to humbly obey the guidelines for living He has established.[2]

---

[1] Ex 3:14
[2] Micah 6:8

With the arrival of Jesus, what it looks like to live in God's house becomes even clearer.

Jesus, the Cornerstone

The Apostle John begins his gospel with a succinct, but revolutionary message: *"The Word became flesh and made his dwelling among us"* (Jn 1:14).

As we keep reading the New Testament, it all comes into focus. Jesus, God's only begotten Son, has come to our world! He is the exact image of the Father's being and all things were made through Him. He has existed for all time and all the fullness of the Godhead is visible in Him.[3] Want to know more about the Father and what it's like to live in His house? Just look and listen to Jesus—*"God the One and Only"* (Jn 1:18).

Toward the end of His life, Jesus makes this very claim: He is the defining reference point for God's house and people. Listen as He teaches in the temple courts – the Parable of the Tenants:

> *"There was a landowner who planted a vineyard. He put a wall around it, dug a winepress in it and built a watchtower. Then he rented the vineyard to some farmers and moved to another place. When the harvest time approached, he sent his servants to the tenants to collect his fruit.*
>
> *"The tenants seized his servants; they beat one, killed another, and stoned a third. Then he sent other servants to them, more than the first time, and the tenants treated them the same way. Last of all, he sent his son to them. 'They will respect my son,' he said.*
>
> *"But when the tenants saw the son, they said to each other, 'This is the heir. Come, let's kill him and take his inheritance.' So, they took him and threw him out of the vineyard and killed him.*

---

[3] John. 1:1-2; I Tim. 3:16; Acts 7:37-38; Philippians 2:5-11; Colossians 1:15-17; 2:9,10; Heb 1:3

"Therefore, when the owner of the vineyard comes, what will he do to those tenants?"

"He will bring those wretches to a wretched end," they replied, "and he will rent the vineyard to other tenants, who will give him his share of the crop at harvest time."

Jesus said to them, "Have you never read in the Scriptures:

"'The stone the builders rejected
  has become the cornerstone;
the Lord has done this,
  and it is marvelous in our eyes'?

Therefore, I tell you that the kingdom of God will be taken away from you and given to a people who will produce its fruit. Anyone who falls on this stone will be broken to pieces; anyone on whom it falls will be crushed."　　　*Mt 21:33-44*

The context of this vignette from Jesus' life was a reoccurring reality: the temple's religious leaders are publicly questioning Jesus' authority (21:23-27). In response, the Master tells three parables and this one is the centerpiece of His teaching. Unlike most of Jesus' parables, this one is clearly allegorical which has led to a host of interpretations. For our purposes, we will focus on the most obvious elements of Jesus' story which are relevant to our theme.

There are multiple characters in this parable. There are farmers or "tenants" who have been dishonest. They have not been faithful to the rental agreement that they had agreed to with the vineyard's owner. There are also servants who represent the owner. They have been sent to collect the rent, but have been repeatedly rejected and killed for their efforts.

Finally, there is the owner's son. As a last-ditch effort, he has been sent by his father to restore relationship with the farmers and collect the past due rent. The landowner's final strategy fails as the tenants knowingly kill his son.

Having set the trap, Jesus turns to the religious leaders present and poses a question: *What is a just response to the tenant's behavior?*

The leaders present knew exactly what should happen: the farmers should be punished and the property given to others who will be faithful. Unknowingly, these religious overseers were condemning themselves and Jesus quotes Psalm 118 to drive the point home.

"The stone the builders rejected has become the cornerstone"! [4]

Jesus is fully aware of the psalm's central theme. Israel has been rejected and mistreated, but there is hope. It has been crushed by its enemies, but God's people will be fully restored. In time, Israel along with their messianic, Davidic-like leader will become an exemplary picture of God's house in all its glory – literally a *"chief corner"* to which the faithful can confidently align their lives.

The religious leaders were not confused by either Jesus' Old Testament reference or His claim. They knew precisely what He meant: I am the fulfillment of the psalmist's prophetic word! I am the rejected son of the vineyard owner; the Son of God Almighty.

Jesus' final affirmation mirrors their condemnation of the tenants: *Therefore, I tell you that the kingdom of God will be taken away from you and given to a people who will produce its fruit (vs. 44).* The religious leaders were furious and began to plot His demise (vs. 45).

Jesus claimed to be the cornerstone – the fixed point – to which God's house should be aligned

---

[4] Builders in biblical times utilized cornerstones to help define plumb as they erected structures. If the walls, floor, and roof were all aligned to this one fixed point, the entire house would be square.

Jesus' Foundational Insights

On another occasion, Jesus leveraged the importance of a house's foundation to make essentially the same point. At the end of His "Sermon on the Mount" (Mt 5:1-7:29), Jesus encouraged His followers to build their life on a trustworthy foundation.

> *Therefore everyone who hears these words of mine and puts them into practice is like a wise man who built his house on the rock. The rain came down, the streams rose, and the winds blew and beat against that house; yet it did not fall, because it had its foundation on the rock. But everyone who hears these words of mine and does not put them into practice is like a foolish man who built his house on sand. The rain came down, the streams rose, and the winds blew and beat against that house, and it fell with a great crash.*
>
> *Mt 7:24-27*

Jesus' concludes His extended sermon with this easy to understand, but power-packed story. He contrasts a house built on permanent stone (His teaching) versus one that is built on unpredictable sand (worldly wisdom). Jesus asserts that the former house will prevail against all storms while the latter will undoubtedly collapse. As residents of wind swept Israel, almost everyone listening would have fully understood this metaphor and therefore, the bold claim He was making.

Peter's Witness

Peter was one of the first to affirm Jesus' identity.

Case in point: Peter and the other apostles are together with Jesus as He continues to teach them about the Kingdom. Jesus wants to get a read on how they are coming along in their learning and He poses a question.

> *When Jesus came to the region of Caesarea Philippi, he asked his disciples, "Who do people say the Son of Man is?"*
>
> *They replied, "Some say John the Baptist; others say Elijah; and still others, Jeremiah or one of the prophets." "But what about you?" he asked. "Who do you say I am?"*
>
> *Simon Peter answered, "You are the Messiah, the Son of the living God." Jesus replied, "Blessed are you, Simon son of Jonah, for this was not revealed to you by flesh and blood, but by my Father in heaven.*   *Mt 16:13-17*

A gold star for Peter! He knows exactly who Jesus is and has the confidence to voice his conviction. Dial forward to the early days after Pentecost in Jerusalem. The number of Jesus followers is exploding and Peter once again boldly proclaims Jesus' identity:

> *Then Peter, filled with the Holy Spirit, said to them: "Rulers and elders of the people! If we are being called to account today for an act of kindness shown to a man who was lame and are being asked how he was healed, then know this, you and all the people of Israel: It is by the name of Jesus Christ of Nazareth, whom you crucified but whom God raised from the dead, that this man stands before you healed. <u>Jesus is "'the stone you builders rejected, which has become the cornerstone.'</u>*   *Acts 4:8-11*

Peter had internalized the Master's claim and now preaches it with clarity. Jesus' life – His words and example—are the definition of Kingdom righteousness to which His followers should all align their lives.

Peter's convictions about Jesus' identity are further clarified in his first letter as he draws from both this Psalm and Isaiah.[5]

As you come to him, the living Stone—rejected by humans but chosen by God and precious to him— you also, like living stones, are being built into a spiritual house to be a holy priesthood, offering spiritual sacrifices acceptable to God through Jesus Christ. For in Scripture it says:
"See, I lay a stone in Zion,
  a chosen and precious cornerstone,
and the one who trusts in him
  will never be put to shame."
 Now to you who believe, this stone is precious. But to those who do not believe,
"The stone the builders rejected
  has become the cornerstone," and,
"A stone that causes people to stumble
  and a rock that makes them fall"   *1 Pt 2:4-11*

Peter is very confident that God is building a spiritual house for His people and its cornerstone is Jesus.

Peter taught that Jesus—the precious Stone— was plumb for God's house

---

Insights from Paul

Apostle Paul was another witness who did not lack confidence in his conviction about Jesus:

By the grace God has given me, I laid a foundation as a wise builder, and someone else is building on it. But each one should build with care. For no one can lay any foundation other than the one already laid, which is Jesus Christ.

1 Cor 3:10,11

There is little doubt that Paul was the premier builder of Christ's Church in his era. Having been commissioned and launched by the Antioch church (Acts 13), he spends the rest of his life planting Jesus houses throughout the Roman empire. As we can see from this early writing, he, like Jesus and Peter, is very clear on the essential starting point for a prevailing community of Christ. It is the Master Himself who serves as the foundation.

In Ephesians, one of Paul's final letters, he unpacks this same truth in more detail including the practical implications of Jesus being the cornerstone of God's house. Let's piece together these revelatory verses that expound on the Jesus' House:

"Consequently, you are no longer foreigners and strangers, but fellow citizens with God's people and also members of his household, built on the foundation of the apostles and prophets, with Christ Jesus himself as the chief cornerstone."

Eph 2:19-20

As Paul writes about God's household, he emphasizes that:

- Jesus is the standard for plumb – the cornerstone – literally the "extreme corner";

- Apostles and prophets lead the formative process. Paul is clearly asserting that affirmed disciples with these spiritual giftings from Jesus (Eph 4:11) are called to catalyze Kingdom-aligned foundations. This is one part of their calling and why I believe they are listed as the first and second giftings within the Church (1 Cor 12:28).

But Paul has more to say:

Although I am less than the least of all the Lord's people, this grace was given me: to preach to the Gentiles the boundless riches of Christ, and to make plain to everyone the administration of this mystery, which for ages past was kept hidden in God, who created all things.   *Eph 3:8-9*

In parallel language to 1 Corinthians 3:10, Paul unpacks his two-fold strategy to establish Christ-aligned foundations for His houses – preaching a redemptive message and driving a godly culture:

- **Jesus' redemptive message.** Building plumb foundations begins with a proclamation of His Good News. This was a consistent first step of Apostle Paul's as he sought to plant churches (i.e. Acts 17:2). Wherever he went, the "boundless riches" of God's grace (Eph 1:7; 2:7-9) was the obvious starting place for laying a foundation. To avoid any confusion, Paul once again clarifies the essential message of the Church:

His (God's) intent was that now, through the church, the manifold wisdom of God should be made known to the rulers and authorities in the heavenly realms, according to his eternal purpose that he accomplished in Christ Jesus our Lord. In him and through faith in him we may approach God with freedom and confidence.   *3:10-12*

Is there a better message?

Jesus is the pathway to amazing and unsearchable grace, and through faith in Him, all people have one-hundred percent full access to the Father, the Lord Almighty. This truth is beyond any treasure I could ever imagine and so much has been said on this subject. And undoubtedly, there is still more to say.[6]

But Paul's second foundational element (vs. 9) is the primary motivation and focus of this book; let's keep going.

- **Jesus' culture of selfless love and equipping-based empowerment.** Paul's second conviction about an enduring, Christ-aligned foundation is simply this: <u>It's not enough for the house of God to be founded only upon propositional truth that defines God's grace. Jesus' House must also be founded upon the values and norms He exemplified: His patient and humble love together with His empowerment of equipped followers.</u>

Where does Paul mention Jesus' *culture* in this passage?

The phrase *"<u>administration</u> of this mystery"* is key to understanding this facet of the foundation. "Administration" and "plan" are the most common English words used to translate Paul's original word oikonomia. Unfortunately, neither of these terms fully capture his intended meaning.

---

[6] God's grace and incarnationally testifying to it was the primary focus of my seminary degree. It is certainly worthy of all the books that have and will be written about it. But my objective with this book is to detail what I did not learn in seminary, namely Paul's second calling: How to oversee Jesus house with His values for selfless love and equipping-based empowerment.

This Greek word combines two parts; oikos (house) and nomia (oversight). Joseph's role in Pharaoh's government (Gen 41:41ff) is an excellent picture of its meaning. As second in command, it was Joseph's responsibility to oversee all segments of Egypt and ensure that they were aligned to Pharaoh's values, expectations and norms. In other words, it was Joseph's role to oversee Pharaoh's "house" by driving his preferred culture. In fact, this was a leadership skill that Joseph had already practiced on a smaller scale in Potiphar's house (Gen 39).

Edgar Schein, a lifelong student of organizations, describes culture as the "sum total of all the shared, taken-for-granted assumptions that a group has learned throughout its history." In other words, culture is the "way things work around here", and is most visible in an organization's rituals, artifacts, and heroes. Indeed, all human organizations — both large and small, new and old—have identifiable cultures that function as behavioral boundaries.

The Heart of the Matter pg. 15

Apostle Paul is claiming to have also been tapped by God to do the same thing: To explain to everyone how His House should be overseen (oikonomia) – an ongoing alignment to Jesus' culture: values, norms and behaviors. As we will see, Paul's subsequent teaching in chapter four of Ephesians proceeds to unpack a Christ-aligned culture in some detail:

1. Jesus' heart for selflessly loving people (4:1-3; 15; 32–5:1) and
2. Jesus' passion for equipping-based empowerment (4:11-16).

Paul taught that alignment to Jesus—the cornerstone —combines His message of grace with His values for selfless love and equipping-based empowerment

For those that learn better with images, here is the blueprint for a Jesus house foundation as I imagine it..

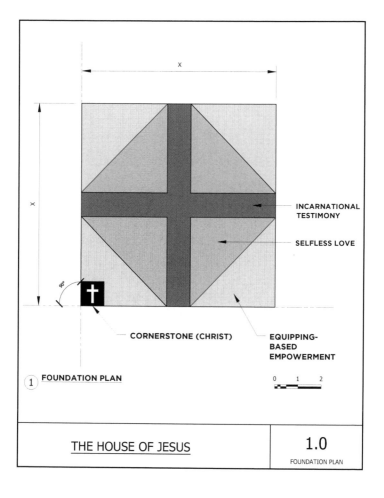

INCARNATIONAL TESTIMONY

SELFLESS LOVE

CORNERSTONE (CHRIST)

EQUIPPING-BASED EMPOWERMENT

① FOUNDATION PLAN

0 1 2

THE HOUSE OF JESUS

1.0

FOUNDATION PLAN

*Corner*formity

I loved working for Bob and Alan; they were great bosses. They were a little crazy as I will explain, but it was a privilege to be a leader under both of them in my mid-thirties.

At the time, they were the visionary and operational leaders of multiple, complimentary businesses. Alan's genius was operational and he hired me to be his assistant. I was fresh out of business school.

One of my first assignments was to conduct a thorough assessment of one of their businesses and determine why it was failing. Within a few weeks, I completed my evaluation, and provided a full report and related recommendations to both. Bottom line: I advised them to make a change at the top of the organization and secure a new General Manager who would exemplify and drive their preferred values and norms.

I felt really good about my findings until the next day: *"Charlie, we really like your analysis and believe you are on target with your suggestions. By the end of the day, we will be making a leadership change and you will be the new General Manager".*

Stunned, scared, shocked, confused, overwhelmed were just a few of the emotions I felt as I walked out the door. Are you guys crazy? I, a complete business novice, am now in charge of a retail and manufacturing business with three locations, 56 employees and 3 million in sales (30+ years ago)?

Long story short, I survived and even thrived. I was not the owner of this company so my role was simply to align the business to Bob and Alan's vision and values. They trusted me to do so and I did it with the help of an fantastic team. Within 18 months, the company had been realigned to the utter amazement of my core leaders and our vendors.

This experience is a great example of *cornerformity*[7]: *conforming a community to its cornerstone.*

It's exactly what Paul is writing about in Ephesians: *helping houses of Jesus conform to what He said (proclaiming His message), who He was (selflessly loving) and what He did (equipping-based empowerment of disciples).*

Ready to unpack the two key elements of Jesus' culture?

Let's start where Paul started: a culture of loving relationships.

---

[7] My new word was inspired by Michael J Gorman's book entitled *Cruciformity: Paul's Narrative Spirituality of the Cross.*

*Corner*formity

Jesus claimed to be the cornerstone—
the fixed point—to which God's house
should be aligned

Peter taught that Jesus—the precious
Stone—was plumb for God's house

Paul taught that alignment to Jesus —
the cornerstone—combines His message
of grace with His values for selfless love
and equipping-based empowerment

90°

THE HOUSE OF JESUS

Section One

Catalyzing a Jesus-aligned, Relational Culture

Key Passages: 1 Cor 13:1-3; John 13-15;
Eph 4:1-3, 32-5:2; Col 3:12-14; Gal 5:22-23

In this section, we will focus on the right first steps for catalyzing a Jesus-aligned culture within His house that single-mindedly prioritizes the ways of God. Since sacrificial love is the defining character trait of God, it is the starting point. As our Father and Jesus model so well, love leads the way.

In the following chapters, we will review what the Bible says about the primacy of love in God's Kingdom (Chapter Three), explore strategies for establishing love-focused values within Jesus' houses (Chapter Four) and, learn how to continually strengthen relational faithfulness (Chapter Five). This section ends with several practical resources including one example of the process (Case Study), a related assessment tool (Culture Survey) and an example of affirmed relational values.

Before we launch into these chapters and topics, however, let me share several convictions that shape the way I view Jesus' house and culture. I believe they will help you stay on track as you keep reading.

The greater a Jesus house is aligned to Him; the greater its Kingdom influence[1]

- The more we replace our thoughts and ways with Jesus', the more we will exemplify His character and influence (Acts 10:28);
- As a Jesus house is increasingly aligned to Him, the more it will also experience the Holy Spirit's power and presence (John 14:15-17, 23-24);
- As a Jesus house intentionally defines and lives out how: 1) His people should interact with one another (loving relationships); and; 2) His community should apprentice and empower anointed servants for His good works (equipping-based empowerment), its ministry initiatives will increasingly produce a meaningful harvest (Luke 8:4-15). This is true for both individual disciples and gathered communities.

No Jesus house has a perfect culture

- The Master's ways are not our ways;
- Every geographical context is marked by deep-seated, worldly values, voices and behaviors that are at war with the Kingdom—arrogance, pride, racism, abuse, control, selfishness, sexism, greed, pragmatism etc. To be sure, some settings are more difficult than others, but every human has been socialized into the world's culture which is toxic within Jesus' house.
- All Jesus communities have some level of divided loyalties—a blend of values from His Kingdom and their surrounding worldly cultures;

---

[1] In my first book, *The Heart of the Matter*, I suggest that the Bible affirms both individual and corporate discipleship. In order to be a Jesus follower, I have to constantly exchange a world where I am the center for a world where God is at the center. It's a daily question of who is in charge. But I also argue that the body of Christ has to make the same choice over and over again. Who is in charge of our gathered community? We, His people, are also invited to deny ourselves, pick up our cross and follow Him!

- Aligning a Jesus community's culture to Him is a never-ending process.

Jesus formed a team of teams to drive His culture

- Jesus modeled the ideal plan: His message and culture are best catalyzed and sustained when spiritually mature, Ephesians 4:11 leaders—Apostles, Prophets, Evangelists, Pastors and Teachers (APEST)—work in unity and share a common leadership language that is aligned to Him. (Ex 18:19-21; Eph 5:1,2; 2 Tim 2:2).

Our Triune God will prevail

- God is more powerful than any culture that opposes Him. *"Who among the gods is like you, Lord? Who is like you— majestic in holiness, awesome in glory, working wonders?"* (Ex 15:11). The entirety of the Bible is crystal clear on this matter: Nothing or no one can prevail against the plans, values, and heart of God (Is 14:27, 46:10-11).

When Jesus is increasingly the center of the church—when Jesus is rightly sitting on the throne in the eyes and hearts of a congregation—the movement of the Spirit is strong, the power of sinful addictions are broken over time, and God's grace is evident to all. At that point, no church leaders, pastors, or laity will have to wonder what to "do" to be a faithful church; Spirit-supplied vitality will ooze out of the pores of that community of disciples.

The Heart of the Matter *(pg. 5)*

90°

Chapter Three

Love Leads the Way

This is how God showed his love among us: He sent his one and only Son into the world that we might live through him. This is love: not that we loved God, but that he loved us and sent his Son as an atoning sacrifice for our sins. Dear friends, since God so loved us, we also ought to love one another.

1 JOHN 4:9-11

In 1976, Mary Lou and I formed a new culture; we got married.

At the time, we didn't describe it that way to others nor did we ever think of it in those terms, but that is exactly what happened. On a day forty two-plus years ago, our personal values, norms and habits began to converge into one, new way of life. The house of Charlie and Mary Lou was born!

At one time, when all three of our sons were at home, our Halley culture was often under the threat of being overthrown! But having prevailed, we now live in harmony with a clear set of norms. Our house's culture clearly outlines how we are to treat one another as well as how we get chores done. In addition, the former (our love for one another) always takes precedence over the latter (our pursuit of shared goals). Relationships taking priority over tasks is not original to the Halley's; it started with God.

Love is God's preeminent value

47

The Father's Example

"For God so loved the world that he gave his one and only Son, that whoever believes in him shall not perish but have eternal life."   *John 3:16*

God's sacrificial love is the reason, motivation, impetus and cause behind His every plan. It drives all of His initiatives. It is also one of the primary differences between the enemy's culture and our Father's—the first and most renowned culture that has ever existed.

The breadth of what the Bible says about God's initiating love is well beyond the scope of this book. But let's take a few minutes to bask in several passages.

The LORD appeared to him from far away. I have loved you with an everlasting love; therefore I have continued my faithfulness to you.   *Jer 31:3*

The Lord is compassionate and gracious, slow to anger, abounding in love. He will not always accuse, nor will he harbor his anger forever; he does not treat us as our sins deserve or repay us according to our iniquities.   *Ps 103:8-10*

But God demonstrates his own love for us in this: While we were still sinners, Christ died for us.   *Romans 5:8*

See what great love the Father has lavished on us, that we should be called children of God! And that is what we are!   *1 John 3:1*

This is how God showed his love among us: He sent his one and only Son into the world that we might live through him. This is love: not that we loved God, but that he loved us and sent his Son as an atoning sacrifice for our sins. Dear friends,

since God so loved us, we also ought to love one another.
1 John 4:9-11

Did you notice in these verses that God's love is the consistent motivation that prompts His grace-filled actions towards us? This amazing love not only saves us from the consequences of our sin, but is the foundation for our new identity as His children! Through faith in Jesus, we can receive the Father's love with freedom and confidence (Eph 3:12). His love explains not only who He is, but what He does and why He does it.

The Father always leads with love

In today's world, however, the word love is ambiguous and can mean lots of different things. To be clear, let me unpack this biblical term more fully by relying on Apostle Paul:

Love is *patient and kind. It does not envy, it does not boast, it is not proud. It does not dishonor others, it is not self-seeking, it is not easily angered, it keeps no record of wrongs. Love does not delight in evil but rejoices with the truth. It always protects, always trusts, always hopes, always perseveres.* *1 Cor 13:4-7*

Love is *joy-filled, peaceful, patient, kind, good, faithful, gentle and self-controlled* *Gal 5:22-23*

Love is *compassionate, kind, humble, gentle and patient* *Col 3:12*

Love *binds them* (all its facets) *all together in perfect unity* *Col 3:14*

Paul has made God's love easier to understand by identifying its many relational facets. It is patient and kind and gentle and humble and compassionate and good and so much more!

Together, these adjectives help us to more fully see the depth and breadth of God's love. Finally, these love-centric values, what Paul calls the "fruit of the Spirit" (Gal 5:22), also instruct you and I on how we are to treat others.

Love Inside the Trinity

It shouldn't be a surprise to learn that love also leads the way within the Trinity. The Bible testifies that God exists as one and as three co-equal persons in relationship. This is reflected in a number of passages that refer to Him in the singular and in the plural:

Then God said, "Let us make mankind in our image, in our likeness…"　　　　　　　　　　　　　　　　　　　*Gen 1:26*

Hear, O Israel: The Lord our God, the Lord is one.　　　*Deut 6:4*

Then I heard the voice of the Lord saying, "Whom shall I send? And who will go for us?"　　　　　　　　　　　　　　*Is 6:8*

Therefore, go and make disciples of all nations, baptizing them in the name of the Father and of the Son and of the Holy Spirit　　　　　　　　　　　　　　　　　　　　　　　*Mt 28:19*

In *Upside Down: The Paradox of Servant Leadership*, Stacy Rinehart highlights that love is the epicenter of the Trinity and serves as the foundation for everything the Father, Jesus and the Holy Spirit does.

"What we see in the Godhead is an incredible picture of interdependence, and unity and diversity, where the One leading and the One being led change according to the need and contribution. Equality is the basis of their relationship…. There is no jealousy or competition in their midst—only harmony and unity. [2]*"*

---

[2] Rinehart, Stacy, *Upside Down: The Paradox of Servant Leadership.* Pg. 88

In no way can this brief section on God's Trinitarian nature do justice to this weighty subject. At the same time, it's vital that we at least affirm that love is not only the essence of Their character, but it's the heart behind everything They accomplish together! We will circle back to their amazing teamwork latter in the book. [3]

Do you see where I am going with all this?

Since love leads the way, catalyzing a Jesus-aligned culture always begins with the cultivation of loving relationships.

Love in the Flesh

For many like myself, our first introduction to God's love was through His Son, Jesus. Give the Father credit; He knew that it would be easier for me and many others to encounter Him by hearing and following a real human being (Jn 1:14). In other words, asking Jesus to be my Lord and Savior was my path to the Father's love and I didn't even know it.

In my earliest years of following Jesus, it was all about Him. It wasn't until I began a daily in-depth reading of the Gospel of John that I began to understand my Heavenly Father.

Jesus gave them this answer: "Very truly I tell you, the Son can do nothing by himself; he can do only what he sees his Father doing, because whatever the Father does the Son also does.

Jn 5:19

Don't you believe that I am in the Father, and that the Father is in me? The words I say to you I do not speak on my own authority. Rather, it is the Father, living in me, who is doing his work.				*Jn 14:10*

---

[3] George Cladis' book *Leading the Team Based Church: How Pastors and Church Staffs can Grow Together into a Powerful Fellowship of Leaders* is an excellent read for those who want to dig deeper into this subject.

> *These words you hear are not my own; they belong to the Father who sent me.*
> *Jn 14:23*

As I witnessed Jesus' affection for those around Him, I gradually began to understand the source of this unconditional love. Jesus and my Heavenly Father are good, gracious, trustworthy and loving (Ps 107:1; Ps 103:8-10); a reality that had never been modeled by my biological father. It was around this time that my first son, Charles, was born and the Father's love became even more tangible.

Charles was born into a student ministry that I was leading at the time. And though Mary Lou and I were his primary caretakers, he had lots of teen-age "moms" and "dads" who also loved to spend time with him. When everyone gathered for our weekly "club" time, Charles was a center of attention and we loved the help!

"Chuck," as he was called, was ten months old on his first Palm Sunday. In advance of that evening's fellowship time, I began to prepare a relevant, gospel message for the students. My original plan was to focus on Jesus' great love and humble sacrifice (Phil 2:5ff). But to my surprise, the talk evolved into a focus on the Father's love: For God so loved the world, He gave His one and only "Chuck." As a young dad, I was tasting the Father's sacrifice from a whole new perspective; it was revelatory.

As I shared that message, I held Charles in my arms and more than a few of the students were powerfully touched by the object lesson, but none more than me. What a watershed week for my heart. Before the creation of the world, my Father chose His "Chuck" to be a perfect sacrifice for my sin (1 Pt 1:20). I will never forget that night.

The process of learning about the depth and breadth of the Father's love continues unabated to this day. Here is a sampling of the kinds of things I keep affirming about God's heart when I read the Gospel of John:

The Father's love is compassionate: *"But whoever drinks the water I give them will never thirst"* (Jn 4:14). Even Samaritan outcasts who have been marginalized by Jewish leaders get to hear the good news.

The Father's love is transformative: *"'Get up! Pick up your mat and walk'. At once the man was cured; he picked up his mat and walked* (John 5:8-9). Years of suffering changes in a moment for a receptive and willing soul.

The Father's love is unexplainable: *"Lazarus, come out!"* (Jn 11:43). Nothing is impossible for God and Jesus does what He sees His Father doing (5:19).

The Father's love is selfless: *"Now that I, your Lord and Teacher, have washed your feet, you also should wash one another's feet. I have set you an example that you should do as I have done for you (Jn 13:14-15).* Jesus serves us humbly; I must follow His example.

Jesus' life is the perfect source for understanding the Father's love

After forty-six years of learning, I appreciate more than ever that Jesus is indeed the *"radiance of God's glory and the exact representation of His being"* (Heb 1:3a). So, everything I have learned and loved about Jesus is also true of the Father as well!

The Apostle's Teaching

What's up with 1 Corinthians 13? Doesn't Paul understand that he needs to stay on point regarding spiritual gifts (Chapter 12) and related ministry issues (Chapter 14)? In fact, positioning these deep truths about the primacy of love and relationships in-between two sections focused on ministry is Spirit-inspired genius! Have you noticed that Paul has a habit of doing this? Every time he mentions spiritual gifts designed to achieve Kingdom visions, he highlights love (see also Rom 12; Eph 4).

Paul's strong convictions in this matter should not surprise us. He is simply restating truths about God that he had discovered in the Old Testament plus what he had received directly from Jesus (Gal 1:12ff). But Paul's stance on the primacy of love is striking: regardless of the capacity of someone's spiritual gifting, there is no benefit to anyone unless it is motivated by godly love (1 Cor 13:1-3). Boom!

Paul's blueprint for Jesus' house also prioritizes love[4]

As I have already highlighted, Paul's strong conviction about a Jesus-aligned houses came, in part, from God's calling on his life as detailed in Eph 3:8-9:

> *Although I am less than the least of all the Lord's people, this grace was given me: to preach to the Gentiles the boundless riches of Christ, and to make plain to everyone the administration of this mystery, which for ages past was kept hidden in God, who created all things.*

Apostle Paul is claiming to have also been tapped by God to explain to everyone how a Jesus-honoring community should internally operate – literally the *"oversight of the house"* (oikonomia).

---

[4] James W. Thompson has written an excellent and comprehensive book on Paul's view of the Church entitled *The Church According to Paul: Rediscovering the Community Conformed to Christ* (2014). He notes that in spite of Paul's inspired teaching on the body of Christ, the Apostle's writings are not embraced by a number of newer church movements that dot the landscape of Christendom (pg. 16).

Here is how I summarize the apostle's dual focus: *Paul's calling was not only to preach Jesus' gospel of grace, but to help everyone understand His culture of love and equipping.*

As we keep reading in Chapter 4, Paul begins to detail Jesus' culture by highlighting the importance of godly relationships. Not surprisingly, love also leads the way within His house!

As a prisoner for the Lord, then, I urge you to live a life worthy of the calling you have received. Be completely humble and gentle; be patient, bearing with one another in love. Make every effort to keep the unity of the Spirit through the bond of peace.   *Eph 4:1-3*

Instead, speak the truth in love   *Eph 4:15*

Be kind and compassionate to one another, forgiving each other, just as in Christ God forgave you. Follow God's example, therefore, as dearly loved children and walk in the way of love, just as Christ loved us and gave himself up for us as a fragrant offering and sacrifice to God.   *Eph 4:32 – 5:2*

In these verses, what facets of love does Paul highlight to instruct the Ephesians on what the relational ideals of Jesus are?

Humility
Gentleness
Patience
Peacemaking
Authenticity
Kindness
Compassion
Forgiving
…..and Christ modeled all of them for us!

Paul establishes a Jesus-aligned foundation of loving relationships (Eph 4:1-3) before he explains Jesus' equipping-based empowerment (Eph 4:11-16)

If any doubt remains regarding Paul's position on the primacy of godly relationships within Jesus' house, listen to his instruction to Timothy. His first letter to this beloved apprentice details a list of qualifications for His household's leaders (1 Tim 3:1-13):

Here is a trustworthy saying: Whoever aspires to be an overseer desires a noble task. Now the overseer is to be above reproach, faithful to his wife, temperate, self-controlled, respectable, hospitable, able to teach, not given to drunkenness, not violent but gentle, not quarrelsome, not a lover of money. He must manage his own family well and see that his children obey him, and he must do so in a manner worthy of full respect. (If anyone does not know how to manage his own family, how can he take care of God's church?) He must not be a recent convert, or he may become conceited and fall under the same judgment as the devil. He must also have a good reputation with outsiders, so that he will not fall into disgrace and into the devil's trap.

In the same way, deacons are to be worthy of respect, sincere, not indulging in much wine, and not pursuing dishonest gain. They must keep hold of the deep truths of the faith with a clear conscience. They must first be tested; and then if there is nothing against them, let them serve as deacons. In the same way, the women are to be worthy of respect, not malicious talkers but temperate and trustworthy in everything.

A deacon must be faithful to his wife and must manage his children and his household well. Those who have served well gain an excellent standing and great assurance in their faith in Christ Jesus.

It's not hard to see Paul's priority for godly relationships, is it? Whether the relationship is within the context of family, business, or public life, the apostle's position is unwavering: disciples are only qualified to lead in Jesus' house if they are being led by love and walking it out.

I agree with the perceptions of Henri Nouwen who questioned how well we have been living into Paul's teaching when he states: *"Much Christian leadership is exercised by people who do not know how to develop healthy, intimate relationships and opted for power and control instead."*[5]

Catalyzing Godly Relationships Today

By now, you may have picked up that I am primarily a practitioner. From studying the Bible and engaging in the trenches of ministry for decades, I have gained a measure of competence in activating and strengthening cultures that desire to honor Jesus. But I am also an observer and admirer of those who have successfully done likewise. Bethel Church in Redding, California is one such Jesus-aligned community.

Danny Silk is a senior leader of Bethel and has done an excellent job capturing the leadership's learnings on relational values. In his book, *Culture of Honor: Sustaining a Supernatural Environment*, he explains one of the key reasons his congregation is renowned for the active movement of God's Spirit within its ministries, particularly as it relates to miracles of healing. In the book's opening paragraph, he states:

> *What you might not have heard is that these supernatural events are directly related to the supernatural culture that the community of saints at Bethel have been developing for over a decade. The heart of the culture is the conviction that Jesus modeled the Christian life for us.*[6]

Silk proceeds to unpack the church's culture of love and its related values: honoring the gifts within the Body; respecting the freedom of believers; being grace-filled in relationships; trusting one another in spite of mistakes; showing generosity towards

---

[5] Henri J. M. Nouwen, *In the Name of Jesus: Reflections on Jesus' Leadership,* Pg. 60.

[6] Silk, Danny, *Culture of Honor: Sustaining a Supernatural Environment*, Pg 29.

all; collaborating within diversity; and prioritizing consistent authenticity.

It's the book of Acts all over again; the interplay of godly relationships and His grace!

> *They devoted themselves to the apostles' teaching and to fellowship, to the breaking of bread and to prayer. Everyone was filled with awe at the many wonders and signs performed by the apostles. All the believers were together and had everything in common. They sold property and possessions to give to anyone who had need. Every day they continued to meet together in the temple courts. They broke bread in their homes and ate together with glad and sincere hearts, praising God and enjoying the favor of all the people. And the Lord added to their number daily those who were being saved.* Acts 2:42-47

Godly relationships catalyze the Gospel of grace

Danny also identifies one other, very important truth that shapes their culture, but you will have to wait for that pearl until Chapter Six!

Love Leads the Way

Love is God's preeminent value

The Father always leads with love

Since love leads the way, catalyzing a Jesus-aligned culture always begins with the cultivation of loving relationships.

Jesus' life is the perfect source for understanding the Father's love

Paul's blueprint for Jesus' house also prioritizes love

Paul establishes a Jesus-aligned foundation of loving relationships (4:1-3) before he explains Jesus' equipping-based empowerment (Eph 4:11-16)

Godly relationships catalyze the Gospel of grace

THE HOUSE OF JESUS

Chapter Four

Establishing Cornerstone Values for Love

For to us a child is born, to us a son is given, and the government will be on his shoulders.And he will be called Wonderful Counselor, Mighty God, Everlasting Father, Prince of Peace. Of the greatness of his government and peace there will be no end. He will reign on David's throne and over his kingdom, establishing and upholding it with justice and righteousness from that time on and forever.   IS 9:6-7

Over my lifetime, I have had the pleasure of partnering with multiple pastors in creating and nurturing Jesus-aligned cultures. Branson Sheets is one of them and on the first Sunday we served together, he hit the nail on the head so to speak. It was his first time preaching in the congregation I had already been serving for three years. He wanted the community to very clearly hear his perspective on Jesus' house and he had three strong convictions he wanted to drive home.

Just before Branson stated his first point, he pulled out a two-by-four wooden board with three partially driven nails in it along with a hammer. As he voiced the initial conviction, he proceeded to smack the first nail and drive it further into the wood.

Bam!

When Branson mentioned his second conviction, he picked up the hammer out again and drove the second nail. Over and over again, he kept highlighting his three priorities and pounding them for thirty-plus minutes. He nailed that sermon!

Obviously, Branson had learned well from Jesus who had a knack for making things easy to understand and remember. Two commandments. One commission. Thirty plus stories. Eight beatitudes. One, geographically-layered vision.

In today's sound bite world, the vast majority of people benefit from a handful of "nails" to help them remember and emulate Jesus' heart for selfless relationships (i.-e. Gal 5:22-23; Col 3:12; Eph 4:1-3). Accordingly, if a Jesus house is serious about establishing His cornerstone priorities for relationships, I suggest they "nail down" three-to-five relational priorities that can be clearly affirmed, taught and modeled (Ex 18:20). In doing so, it sets the stage for these values to be learned, internalized and transferred within and beyond the community.

Cornerstone relational values accelerates alignment to Jesus

I will admit that there are times when charismatic leaders —who embody Jesus' relational values—intuitively catalyze communities toward His ideals. But what happens when they are gone? And how about all the community participants who are not able to decode their lives and words? Clearly understood, stated and affirmed relational values allow all of us to articulate the nature of Jesus' house, embed these values in others and hold each other accountable.

As previously highlighted, apostles and prophets ideally establish these foundational values from the outset of a Jesus house just as Paul did (Eph 2:19-20). When this does not happen, however, there is a need to go back and re-found them.[1]

An Example of Re-Founding

At forty-seven, I began an eight-year journey as one of the senior leaders within a large congregation.[2] This was not a new role for me; I had served another Jesus house with essentially the same responsibilities. What made this job distinctive was the community's need to be *re-founded.*

When the congregation was initially launched, its founders had done a good job of establishing a clear message of grace (Eph 2:7-9). Everyone agreed it was a strength and it had become the focus of the community's worship, preaching and discipleship. Many people experienced saving faith through this community. However, a Jesus-aligned culture of love and equipping-based empowerment (Eph 3:9, 4:1-16, 4:32–5:2) had never been clearly defined or intentionally modeled by the leadership. Not surprisingly, this vacuum of clarity was then filled by a patchwork of values that included secular priorities and institutional habits.

A vacuum of Kingdom-culture clarity is usually filled by worldly values

My initial priority in that congregation was straight-forward, but not easy: facilitate a refounding process to enable the leaders and as many disciples as possible to embrace Jesus' values. Given my life experiences and understanding of Paul (1 Cor 13:1-3),

---

[1] I have not been able to confirm which organizational development writer popularized this term, but "refounding" means just what you would expect. Some entities are not initially established in a way that fully allows them to achieve their dreams and destiny. In these situations, the best, long-term solution is to press pause and "refound" the organization. It typically begins with adding more depth and breadth to the organization's written ideology; its "DNA". In so doing, the foundational identity of the entity is clarified and strengthened which then sets the stage for a season of rigorous alignment and revitalization.

[2] My title was Executive Director and my primary roles were Head of Staff and Director of Ministry.

I knew that establishing Jesus' values of love was the starting point. I recommended a bottom-up and multi-phased strategy that would inspire disciples to learn and leaders to codify Jesus' heart for people. A "Soil Prep Team"[3] was formed and they partnered with me to guide the way. The key desired outcome of the process was to summarize Jesus' heart for relationships through a handful of core values.

After about six months, the following four relational values were affirmed by leadership consensus:

Worshipful Living
A dedication to passionate devotion and intentional obedience
Jesus said that the Father is seeking those who worship Him in Spirit and in Truth. We must practice a life of worship that invites the presence of Jesus into all that we are and do.

Humble Service
A calling to be generous towards God and others
Jesus came to serve, not to be served. He modeled a servant life not only with His disciples, but also with society's lost, outcast and oppressed. Accordingly, we follow His example.

Authentic Relationships
A commitment to respect and integrity
Jesus' relationships were honest and genuine. We too are compelled to relate honestly with those inside and outside the church. In so doing, we are refreshed and encouraged by our love for one another.

Loving Compassion
A command to look beyond ourselves
Jesus looked at broken humanity through the eyes of love and compassion and came to give His life away. We are called to see

---

[3] Think Jesus' Parable of the Soils!

the world from God's perspective and give ourselves away as messengers of salvation, hope and healing.[4]

Each of these relational values included multiple supporting Bible verses and were graphically depicted as one part of God's heart. In time, examples of what these priorities did and did not mean were added.

There is no way to precisely quantify the impact of this process to define Jesus' standards for relationships. What I can say is that the community grew both in spiritual depth and missional breadth while I was a leader, and is continuing to thrive eight years after my departure. In the next chapter, I will detail how we sustained and strengthened these relational values within the community once they were in place.

Multiple Options for Refounding

There is more than one way to refound Jesus' values. One option is for a handful of core influencers to make it happen.[5] The benefit of this approach is the speed with which the values can be defined and shared. The challenge? If the larger community does not participate in the process, it can sometimes be difficult for them to fully embrace and own the leadership's recommendation.

Another and contrasting option is a bottom-up approach which seeks to include as many as possible in the process. (This option is detailed below.) As you would expect, this strategy's benefits and costs are the opposite of the first. It takes a lot more time to get the values written and affirmed, but once accomplished, community buy-in is well on its way to being accomplished.

---

[4] See another example of relational values after Chapter 5.

[5] Checkout the Modesto Manifesto that Billy Graham and his core team crafted as they started their ministry together.

Leaders are encouraged to carefully assess their community's spiritual maturity and expectations before finalizing how much they will participate in the process.[6]

There is no right way to refound Jesus' values within an established community

Regardless of the strategy chosen, here are several relevant principles to honor as the process unfolds:

Begin Refounding Only After Securing Core Leadership Consensus: Don't move forward until all the essential stakeholders within the community understand and are onboard regarding both the desired outcomes and related steps of the process.

Get Ready to Learn Patience: No matter what strategy is embraced to define its relational core values, it's going to take time. If you are the facilitator, recognize and remember that Jesus is glorified when we honor one another along the way. At the end of the process, it is important to be able to say: *"It seemed good to the Holy Spirit and to us"* (Acts 15:28).

Get Ready for a Spiritual Battle: Apostle Paul knew that implementing his foundational strategies (what Jesus said, was and did) would be a spiritual battle for any community that followed his counsel. Ephesians 6:10-16 captures this clearly: our struggle to take a stand for Jesus' values is not about flesh and blood, but a battle with demonic forces. Believe it and lead accordingly!

---

[6] Please process the principle *"Honor the Existing Culture"* below and note its comment about controllers as you discern which route is best for your community.

Insights on a Bottom-Up Approach

What follows are convictions, stories and resources designed to assist community leaders who are proceeding with a broad-based approach to learning and defining core values for relationships. Most of these how-to strategies were utilized in the example detailed above, but not all. Their order generally reflects the ideal sequence, but there are many places of overlap and sometimes lots of repetition is needed.

Define the Win in Advance: People need help seeing the destination. So, it makes sense to share an example of what a finished set of relational values looks like and why the process is important. (Check out the 10 Commandments and its relational focus! Or the fruit of the Spirit in Galatians 5:22-23.) At the same time, beware that some results-oriented leaders may be tempted to copy the work of another Jesus house and move on. Avoid that temptation! The process is essential for many to learn what the Bible says and own the outcome.

Form a Guiding Team: An oversight team creates an additional opportunity to train leaders as well as build credibility. Ideally, an experienced coach can be secured to resource the team. Finding this kind of a "cornerstone coach" can be a game changer. Overall, the team should focus on widening ownership, building leadership consensus and capturing it in print (Acts 15).

Prepare Hearts to Begin: Any initiative that emphasizes a community's learning from God's Word as well as a shift of culture naturally makes corporate prayer, worship and fasting strategic starting points. These spiritual disciplines are highly effective in preparing hearts to receive Jesus' truth. Indeed, these disciplines are central avenues by which God communicates with and shapes His people.

Prioritize Wide Ownership: A bottom-up process is slower and messier, but it offers great benefits. One is wide ownership of the outcome and the community's future. Getting a high percentage of stakeholders involved greatly enhances their enthusiasm for living out the relational values once they are in place.

Keep Emphasizing Learning, Not Deciding: My hope is that Jesus communities would approach this process as a focus on learning (a spiritual exercise) rather than deciding (a worldly exercise). As citizens of God's Kingdom, we are servants, and as such, we are to learn His design for our lives. We should always be asking what is important to Him. Regrettably, many communities adopt secular models for crafting these foundational definitions which prioritizes what <u>we</u> think is important.

Link the Process to Existing Groups: Include some special events to rally people toward the goal. Most of the process, however, can be accomplished in whatever groups already exist within the body that include the community's weekly gatherings for worship, discipleship dyads, small groups, regular classes etc. Design the process to intentionally plug into the discipleship strategies already in place!

Focus on Jesus' Ideals, Not Current Norms: The fruit of the Spirit is not a description of my life; far from it. Rather they are the ideals that Jesus has called me to press on towards (Phil 3:14-16). Be aware that secular organizations tend to affirm values that already exist within their culture. This process, however, is intended to affirm Jesus' perfect character not our reality.

Honor the Community's Established Culture and Leaders: As much as possible, the process should honor the existing culture and leaders of the community. (Exceptions to this rule do exist, particularly in places dominated by leaders with controlling tendencies.) In other words, the process should recognize and work within any process boundaries already in place. Obviously, a failure to honor existing norms tends to de-legitimize the entire exercise.

Customize Whatever Model You Adopt: There are multiple strategies for mobilizing a community to identify and affirm Jesus' values.[7] Cataloging all of Paul's love-focused adjectives followed by a forced-choice strategy together with multiple layers of team processing is a common way to arrive at a core list of three to five.[8] As you use any model, always be ready to make adjustments to fit your context.

Surprised by Thorny Weeds

When I first began to serve in ministry, I was SO naïve!

I just assumed that all Jesus houses would align themselves to His godly values. In other words, I expected all of His houses to be planted in "good" soil per His *Parable of the Soils* (Luke 8:4-15),

Remember His allegory?

Jesus explained that a fourth type of soil is "good" and represents single-minded people whose hearts are receptive and willing. And when the Gospel seed is planted within them, the harvest is expansive: thirty-, sixty- and a hundred-fold.

Unfortunately, it took me very little time to discover that most Jesus houses over the centuries have resided in the third, tainted soil—communities of disciples with divided loyalties. At one time, these people had been receptive to God, but subsequently got derailed by their ongoing love of worldly values—the familiar

---

[7] At present, I believe Tom Bandy's model detailed in his book *Moving Off the Map* is one of the most comprehensive of these strategies and can easily be tweaked to fit most houses.

[8] A forced-choice process is one simple way to move from a large number of values to four to six. An example: If you identify 32 facets of love, utilize multiple groups to boil these down to four through several steps—go from 32 to 16 and then to 8 and then to 4. Gather all the "4 lists", share them with leadership groups and have them reduce all values listed to their top 4. The Planning Team then finalizes the process and writes a draft for review.

and thorny voices of the surrounding culture. In Jesus' story, the viability of their faith is choked by their waffling commitment and their harvest is inconsequential.

I am no longer naïve.

Today, I am fully aware that the absence of clarity about Jesus' relational values creates a vacuum that the enemy loves to fill with his own norms and behaviors (Rom 12:2; Col 2:8; Is 55:8-13). But learning, writing and affirming Jesus' relational values is the easy part.

It is now time to unpack the more difficult and ongoing process of alignment.

Establishing a Foundation of Love

Cornerstone relational values
accelerates alignment to Jesus

A vacuum of Kingdom-culture clarity
is usually filled by worldly values

There is no right way to refound Jesus'
values within an established community

Begin Refounding Only After
Securing Core Leadership Consensus

Get Ready to Learn Patience

Get Ready for a Spiritual Battle

90°

THE HOUSE OF JESUS

Chapter Five

Aligning a Community to Love

You must be the people's representative before God and bring their disputes to him. Teach them His decrees and instructions, and show them the way they are to live and how they are to behave. But select capable men from all the people—men who fear God, trustworthy men who hate dishonest gain—and appoint them as officials over thousands, hundreds, fifties and tens. EX. 18:19-21

Patience may be a virtue, but in the twenty-first century, it seems to be more and more rare. The vast majority of us want what we want now, which really stands for **no other wa**y: not later, not tomorrow, but now.

It's also my observation that many of today's Christians want spiritual maturity "now." As if they could cozy up to their computers, access **www.JesusHouse.com** and click on the *Discipleship* icon. Once there, they could then select *Personal* followed by *Immediate* from the drop-down menu. Voila! They are changed instantly into a combination of Mother Teresa and Billy Graham, ready to take on the world, their family and job. If only our heart transformation was that easy! But it is not. Jesus never expected it to be.

And while we are at it, why don't we sanctify the communities of faith we reside in? We'll just go back to the home page and click on *Corporate* followed by *Immediate*. How great would that be!

Our community would instantly be transformed into an amazingly fertile, Soil #4 culture that walks out Jesus-aligned relational values and witnesses exceptional harvests!

As I am sure you already know, being a disciple of Jesus is a lifelong process of alignment to His heart that bears no resemblance to this "now" mindset. It is not just a decision; a timed and dated event; an isolated, life-changing experience that happened some years ago; or even a certain span of years when God seemed nearby. Rather, it's an ongoing walk of faith towards His Kingdom — a place where God fully reigns within and among us.

Until now, my focus on a Jesus-aligned culture has been more conceptual: How does the Father's love inform how we are to live life together? and How do we establish Jesus' values and norms for godly relationships within His house?

It is now time to tackle more practical questions regarding alignment: *How can the influencers of a Jesus house be trained to become value carriers for His relational culture? and What is the best way to empower them to embed Jesus' heart for selfless love throughout His house?*

Jethro's Alignment Strategies

Wow!

Initially, Jethro was more than impressed as Moses detailed God's deliverance of Israel from the hand of Pharaoh (Ex 18:7ff). This priest of Midian and father of Moses' wife Miriam was profoundly impacted by his son-in-law's testimony and declares: *"Now I know that the Lord is greater than all other gods"* (vs. 11). Inspired by what he has heard, Jethro responds with heart-felt offerings: a festive celebration of God's goodness while also honoring Israel's first family and the nation's seventy Elders.

Wow!

The next day, however, is a different story. Jethro is troubled and dismayed by what he is seeing (vs. 13-16). All day long, he observes Moses serving as the sole arbiter for a nation of six-hundred thousand or so men and their families. Really? Jethro's response is once again swift and on the mark: *"What you are doing is not good. You and these people who come to you will only wear yourselves out. The work is too heavy for you; you cannot handle it alone"* (vs. 17-18).

Fortunately, Jethro has a clear picture of the desired outcome:

"You must be the people's representative before God and bring their disputes to him. Teach them His decrees and instructions, and show them the way they are to live and how they are to behave. But select capable men from all the people—men who fear God, trustworthy men who hate dishonest gain—and appoint them as officials over thousands, hundreds, fifties and tens." (vs. 19-21)

Genius!

This is an example of a decentralized and layered leadership structure where every influencer is a carrier of God's values, norms and behaviors. With surgical precision, the Bible's first organizational consultant delivers Kingdom wisdom for Moses on the how to's of discipling Israel's influencers *(pray, teach, show)* and placing them within a sustainable leadership structure *(1,000s, 100s, 50s and 10s)*.

Moses humbly accepts Jethro's council and a full-scale reorganization ensues. While the Old Testament does not tell us exactly how this realignment process unfolded, the New Testament details another, relevant example. It's time to learn from the genius of the Master!

How Jesus Catalyzed His Values of Love

Jesus was born into Israel's history at a time of extreme brokenness and hopelessness. Was it even possible that any person and/or strategy could catalyze a new, Kingdom-centric culture during these discordant times? Could this new movement also be aligned to God's heart for relationships, and ultimately make a lasting impact on the world? Yes. That is exactly what happened.

How did this reality come to be? And what can we learn from Jesus' ways that will inform and accelerate our efforts to sustain alignment to His relational ideals?

Let's review Jesus' life through the lens of Jethro's transformational process and see what we glean.

Pray

Very early in the morning, while it was still dark, Jesus got up, left the house and went off to a solitary place, where he prayed.
Mk 1:35

One of those days Jesus went out to a mountainside to pray, and spent the night praying to God. When morning came, he called his disciples to him and chose twelve of them, whom he also designated apostles.
Lk 6:12-13

One day Jesus was praying in a certain place. When he finished, one of his disciples said to him, "Lord, teach us to pray, just as John taught his disciples."
Luke 11:1

These words you hear are not my own; they belong to the Father who sent me.
John 14:24

They went to a place called Gethsemane, and Jesus said to his disciples, "Sit here while I pray." He took Peter, James and John along with him, and he began to be deeply distressed and troubled. "My soul is overwhelmed with sorrow to the point of death," he said to them. "Stay here and keep watch." Going a little farther, he fell to the ground and prayed that if possible the hour might pass from him. Mk 14:32-35

See also Lk 18:1; 22:39-41; Mt 6:9-10; Jn 5:19; 17:1

The book of Acts states that Jesus healed all who were under the power of the evil one because His Father was with Him (Acts 10:38).

So why was God with Jesus?

The Father makes His home within all who trust Him with a child-like heart (Mt 4:1-11; 18:3; John 14:22). That is exactly what Jesus did and it positioned Him to walk in the Father's strength, affirmation, wisdom and divine strategies. In other words, Jesus' character and capacity flowed from His intimate communion with and dependence upon the Father through abiding prayer. It was the lifeblood of Jesus' daily existence and is the explanation of His supernatural power (Jn 14:10).

It is no different for any Kingdom citizen today who desires to live the same impactful life. Like Moses, we, too, must prayerfully position ourselves before God—Father, Son and Holy Spirit—and welcome Their life-giving presence. This is the holy place where we experience transformational intimacy with the Father as well as receive the Holy Spirit's power to love and serve others (John 14:15-17). These truths are especially relevant for those God calls to lead out as apostles, prophets, evangelists, pastors and teachers (Eph 4:11). In other words, the transformation of a Jesus house's culture hinges on the heart transformation of its leaders. Unless Christ-like love is flowing from their abiding relationship in Him, nothing of lasting significance can happen (1 Cor 13:1-3).

Intimacy with God is the starting point for realigning a culture to love

Teach

Again Jesus began to teach by the lake. The crowd that gathered around him was so large that he got into a boat and sat in it out on the lake, while all the people were along the shore at the water's edge. Mk 4:1

With many similar parables Jesus spoke the word to them, as much as they could understand. Mk 4:33

When the Sabbath came, he began to teach in the synagogue, and many who heard him were amazed. Mk 6:2

And beginning with Moses and all the Prophets, he explained to them what was said in all the Scriptures concerning himself.
Lk 24:27

Then he left the crowd and went into the house. His disciples came to him and said, "Explain to us the parable of the weeds in the field." Mt 13:36

See also Mark 2:1,2; Mt 5:1; Jn 7:14

Having received the fullness of His Father's love, Jesus taught on the primacy of love with authority. The crowds were hungry for His boldness and clarity, something they had never heard. Jesus goes so far as to claim that freedom flows from obedience to His teaching: *"If you hold to my teaching, you are really my disciples. Then you will know the truth, and the truth will set you free* (Jn 8:31,32). Boom!

But Jesus does not stop there; He's just beginning. The goal of His ministry? To destroy the works of the enemy (1 Jn 3:8)—the source of the world's lies (Jn 8:44). So, it should not surprise us that teaching was one of His primary strategies to reignite a Kingdom-centric culture.

Jesus' style of communicating truth, however, is so much more than today's classroom and online learning paradigms. He shared Kingdom truth on relationships as He lived life: wherever he went, whoever He was with and whatever the context. Jesus' teaching ministry began with the crowds, but evolved over time. As His ministry progressed, He focused more and more time confiding in three, training the Twelve, and equipping the seventy to partner with Him. With all, He shared the keys to godly relationships through transferable stories, Old Testament passages, asking great questions and highlighting daily events. You name it and He leveraged it to shed light on loving one another. He claimed to be the Light of the world and He was!

For Jesus house leaders today, explaining God's Word in regards to Kingdom relationships is a powerful way to combat the destructive force of worldly norms. By doing this in conjunction with already affirmed Jesus-aligned relational values, disciples more easily learn how let go of the enemy's lies and embrace godly ways.

Helping disciples learn and obey God's Word accelerates alignment towards Jesus' values

Show

The Word became flesh and made his dwelling among us.

John 1:14

While Jesus was having dinner at Levi's house, many tax collectors and sinners were eating with him and his disciples, for there were many who followed him. *Mk 2:15*

While Jesus was in one of the towns, a man came along who was covered with leprosy. When he saw Jesus, he fell with his face to the ground and begged him, "Lord, if you are willing, you can make me clean. Jesus reached out his hand and touched the man."

Lk 5:12

Just then his disciples returned and were surprised to find him talking with a woman. But no one asked, "What do you want?" or "Why are you talking with her?" Jn 4:27

When they had all had enough to eat, he said to his disciples, "Gather the pieces that are left over. Let nothing be wasted." So they gathered them and filled twelve baskets with the pieces of the five barley loaves left over by those who had eaten. Jn 6:12-13

About eight days after Jesus said this, he took Peter, John and James with him and went up onto a mountain to pray. Lk 9:28

See also Mt 14:29; Jn 11:38, 21:15.

Modeling is the most powerful form of teaching. So it should not be a surprise that Jesus became a man, lived with us and showed everyone what godly relationships and selfless love looks like. In the Gospel examples just highlighted, He...

- Validates people trapped in sin by eating with them;
- Provides a clear picture of compassion by breaking with tradition and touching a leper;
- Honors a woman publicly and sends a clear, but unexpected message to His followers;
- Incorporates His key leaders into a miracle of fish and loaves so they can see it firsthand;
- Models prayer for His three key leaders.

Bottom line: Jesus' life was an open book for all to see and through it, He wrote volumes (Jn 21:25)! Obviously, the Master understood that the relational culture He was touting would be validated more by who He was than what He said. Anyone could argue with His claims and affirmations, but His actions and spiritual power would be more difficult to dispute.

This same reality remains true for today's Kingdom teachers and leaders. The people of our communities are more inspired by

God's relational work in our hearts than our accrued knowledge. Wendy Backland says it so well: *"No one wants to know what you know until they want what you have".[1]* So when intimacy with God combines with sound teaching and lives aligned to love, momentum builds for a Kingdom culture.

Walking the teaching talk accelerates culture shifts towards love

Select

One of those days Jesus went out to a mountainside to pray, and spent the night praying to God. When morning came, he called his disciples to him and chose twelve of them, whom he also designated apostles.   Lk 6:12-13

Jesus went up on a mountainside and called to him those he wanted, and they came to him. He appointed twelve that they might be with him and that he might send them out to preach and to have authority to drive out demons.   Mk 3:13

Calling the Twelve to him, he began to send them out two by two and gave them authority over impure spirits.   Mk 6:7

After this the Lord appointed seventy-two others and sent them two by two ahead of him to every town and place where he was about to go. He told them, "The harvest is plentiful, but the workers are few. Ask the Lord of the harvest, therefore, to send out workers into his harvest field.   Lk 10:1-2

Jesus' strategy for securing the right influencers tracks closely with Jethro's wise council to Moses: *call out group influencers who demonstrate godly character.* Jesus knew that future leaders of His

---

[1] A quote from Steve and Wendy Backlund's presentation to the Antioch Discipleship School (Waco, TX) in early 2011.

House would need to model love for God and one another (Jn 15:5-8; 1 Cor 13:1-3).[2]

The weight of choosing apostles with the right character was so large, it became the focus of an extended night of prayer for Jesus. He needed wisdom from His Father to move forward. Once these apostles were in place and apprenticed as just detailed, He chose additional disciples with godly character (i.-e. the 70 from Lk 10) to be value carriers who would also pray, teach, show and select others.

Inviting the right like-hearted disciples to lead God's people is as important today as it was for Jesus. Which is why He implored us to pray accordingly: *"Ask the Lord of the harvest, therefore, to send out workers into his harvest field"* (Lk 10:2). Jesus (and Jethro) have a sound selection plan: prayer, teaching, and modeling that highlights leaders with proven character.

Jesus' relational values become daily norms as godly value-carriers are prayed for, taught, apprenticed and selected

A New Term: *Heart Discipleship*

The Jesus process I have just detailed is the essence of what I call "heart discipleship". It may not be original, but it's how I capture the process of training a Jesus follower to receive God's love and walk it out relationally. It is typically a life-on-life process with 2-4 people that is gender specific and focused on topics like spending time with God, how to understand His Word, loving others, spiritual disciplines, spiritual warfare etc. These groups are a perfect setting for accountability as well as raising up and releasing new disciplers.[3] In Chapter Eight, I will detail *ministry discipleship* which focuses on cultivating a disciple's spiritual gifts and ministry capacity.

---

[2] I do understand that Saul (later Paul) is an obvious contradiction to the principle I am touting, but I'm OK with Jesus making the exception. How He picked the 12 seems to be the norm for today's leaders!

[3] Check out "life transformation groups" in Neil Cole's book *Organic Church*. A great model for heart discipleship.

Organizing Value Carriers Like Jesus

The vast majority of leaders, like myself, can relate to Moses being overwhelmed by his responsibilities and working from "morning to evening" (Ex 18:13). In frenetic times like these, I have felt like a hamster on a running wheel. I try to accomplish more by running faster, but make no additional progress. And so, I, like Moses, welcome Jethro's decentralized strategy to mobilize trained leaders. It's the only way to escape the wheel: smarter beats faster every day!

It's no surprise then, that from the outset, Jesus would implement a Jethro-inspired structure to sustain His up-and-coming value carriers – the 3, 9, 70 and 420.[4]

- The 3 were Peter, James and John; His key value carriers to the 9 and beyond;[5]
- The 9 were the rest of the Apostles; also vital catalysts with a 70 focus;
- The 70 men were a third layer of faithful carriers (Lk 10); essential truth and culture carriers to hundreds after Pentecost;
- The 420 is everyone else who Jesus touched after the resurrection and before His ascension; a variety of men and woman who were undoubtedly movement founders before (Acts 1:12-15) and after Pentecost.

What follows are macro-lessons I have learned from a lifetime of striving to emulate Jesus' heart discipleship of influencers within a leadership structure designed to sustain them.

---

[4] Don't interpret Jesus' leadership structure as rigid, but as an example of a layered and reproducible strategy. FYI: My 420 comes from the 500 who saw Jesus after His resurrection and before His ascension minus the 12 and 70 (and rounded for ease of teaching).

[5] I found this fascinating: Alexander of Clement, the 2nd century theologian wrote, ""The Lord after his resurrection imparted knowledge to James the Just and to John and Peter, and they imparted it to the rest of the apostles, and the rest of the apostles to the seventy, of whom Barnabas was one." The reference is the church father Eusebius' "ECCLESIASTCAL HISTORY, BOOK." VII. ii. 1. http://www.earlychristianwritings.com/text/clement-fragments.html

With Core Influencers like Peter, James and John

Over my decades of ministry, the 3 have been my closest colleagues in ministry. They are people I would and did entrust my life to. The vast majority have been very different than I in regards to background, experience and spiritual gifting, but Solomon was right: *"Two are better than one for they have a good return for their labor"* (Eccl 4:9-12). In spite of geographic moves, I have lost track of only a few of these brothers and sisters over the years, and still pray weekly for many of them.

Disciple the 3: As has already been stated, modeling is the most powerful form of teaching and it always begins with the overseers of any movement, community, ministry or team. I have spent countless hours studying and meditating on what the Scriptures say about Kingdom relationships (i.e. Proverbs) and asking the Spirit to help me "teach and show" these truths to core influencers.[6] This process has transformed me from the inside out and is always the first priority.

Constantly Be on the Lookout for Peter, James and John Value Carriers: Jesus, Paul and many others highlight the essential need for partners in ministry. Look around you: Great teams are led by great sub-teams. I'm always on the lookout for new partners to invest in and raise up. And as already stated, find your key influencers by using character as your primary filter.

Model to the 3 as You Invest in the 9: Apprenticing your Peter, James and John in the affirmed relational values demands that they watch you live them out and equip others. Be attentive to this reality and always be thinking of how this core can be a part of your week.

Honor Core Influencers with One-on-One Time: Making regular, one-on-one relational investments in your key leaders

---

[6] When my core influencers were women, I did not heart disciple them, but I did ask them questions so that I could better understand how I could pray for them and what they needed. I would then network them with other mentors accordingly.

builds a foundation of trust that is essential for accomplishing God honoring visions. Remember: Love leads the way. Accordingly, be attentive to the love language of your core disciples. What "put ins" are most impactful for each? Peter was very different than John!

Build a Common Language among Core Influencers: The core team is where a shared leadership language begins and I suggest starting by memorizing key, relational passages together. Leverage God's Word to build defining phrases, slogans, statements and narratives. This is much more powerful than mimicking the DNA of other faith communities. The process of creating together catalyzes stronger ownership.

Establish a Culture of Feedback: A hunger for greater relational faithfulness is a value that starts at the top and works its way down through a community. That being the case, this lead team needs to be pacesetters at fostering a culture that prioritizes feedback and accountability. The old adage is true: *Don't ask others to do what you are unwilling to do yourself.*

With Strategic Equippers like The Other Apostles

Whereas my "Peter, James and John" were those I mentored myself, these 3 initially partnered with me to disciple the 9 "other apostles". My journey in ministry has not led me to spend a lifetime in one place, but if it had, many of these up and coming 9 would have become core influencers right beside me. I am very proud of these brothers and sisters, and did my best to give them a strong foundation in ministry. Here are a few ways I sought to be attentive to their needs and potential.

Equip the 9 Along with the 3: Sometimes it makes the most sense to teach all 12 at the same time. It's an essential strategy to build and sustain momentum towards embedding relational values into your culture, and as able, ask the core 3 to help out. Be attentive to the learning styles of your team and seize relevant opportunities to teach via devotions, recognition, daily events, conflict, dysfunction, conferences and focused studies.

Drive Transferable Language: Expect these 9 strategic leaders to also memorize relational values, transferable slogans and relevant passages. Understanding these baseline truths is beneficial, but more importantly, these leaders need to be prepared to give them away to others. Emulate the process by which medical doctors are trained as they "see one, do one and teach one". Observing, practicing and sharing is also the process by which disciples become and multiply relational value carriers.

Assume that Your Strategic Equippers Need to Grow as Communicators: This assumption comes from years of working with many adults who grew up in dysfunctional homes. Don't we all need to improve our skill on interpersonal communication—the primary medium of love? When I served as the point person for ministry in a large church, every year I taught my new staff the basics of effective listening and speaking to others. This 8-week process grounded in Proverbs was a great way for them to learn our culture and get ready to model excellence for others. Reread 1 Cor 13:1-3 and believe it!

Expect Your Strategic Equippers to "Leak" Vision: Leaders easily lose sight of their community's vision and priorities. Therefore, it's essential to keep repeating the vision for a culture of Kingdom relationships over and over again. The way I and many pastors were trained to preach works well with vision casting too: *tell them what you are going to tell them, tell them and tell them what you told them.*

Position the 9 to Influence the 70: From my vantage point, Jesus leveraged the 3 to help Him apprentice and mobilize the 9 as Kingdom value carriers. Accordingly, I see the same process unfolding with the 70: the 9 are equipped and empowered in the Jesus way to teach and show the 70 what Jesus-aligned relationships looks like.

With Maturing Influencers like The Seventy

In my early years in vocational ministry, I was a "seventy" disciple. I had been spotted by strategic equippers and was discipled by them. In this season, they strengthened my relational wisdom and understanding of Jesus' values. How grateful I am for their investment in me and helping me to grow into my destiny.

As you are seeing, I partnered with my 3 to train the 9 so they could spot and invest in this leadership segment and resource them accordingly. At times, I would be the one to identify a future Eph 4 equipper within the 70 and be their discipler, but that was the exception, not the rule. My focus has always been to help leaders at one level develop leaders at the next.

Be Attentive to the 70: Jesus' primary focus was unequivocally developing the three and the twelve, but He recognized the importance of investing in the 70 (Luke 10). Decentralizing leadership demands that upfront leaders have face time with each level of influencers; it's one of their most important roles.

Always Be on the Lookout for Future Apostles: The next generation of "apostles" will come from the ranks of the seventy. Indeed, the 3, 12, 70 and 420 are linked by a dynamic pipeline that allows leaders to move from one level of leadership to the next in keeping with their faithfulness and anointing. The goal is to help each of them walk out their destiny as Kingdom influencers.

Equip the 70 to Influence the 420: As already highlighted, upfront teaching, preaching and messaging is very important to driving values among faithful followers, but nothing beats the power of heart discipleship (2-4 people). As already noted, life-on-life impartation of truth – apprenticing—is the most powerful form of teaching there is.[7]

---

[7]   I highly recommend the book *Exponential: How You and Your Friends can Start a Missional Movement* by Dave and Jon Ferguson for those want to dig deeper into the art of apprenticing.

Intentionally Message with This Audience: This leadership strata needs to hear the same, upfront core messaging from senior leaders regarding Kingdom relationships, but it will inevitably be more concise and less often. Establish a sustainable rhythm of visibility and communication with these servants based on their needs and the realities of the community. It builds unity as these top three levels of leadership all move together towards a common relational vision. A word to core influencers: Disciplined repetitiveness with the seventy is more important and difficult than most realize.

With the Faithful Followers like The Four-Hundred Twenty

As I am sure you already understand, l was also a "420" disciple at one time. l was young in the faith and desperately needing the help of a "70" discipler in order to faithfully follow Jesus. Again, I am thankful for the men that came around me in these years; I can't imagine where I would be today without them.

As a senior leader, here are a few ways in which I sought to supplement the ministry of the 70 to the 420.

Assume New Participants have Never Experienced Jesus' Relational Values: My decades of experience suggest that it is not safe to assume that the newer participants in your community have ever experienced Jesus' relational norms as I have been describing. In thirty plus years of ministry, I have met only a small number of people who were fluent in how to listen actively, speak effectively and resolve conflict "in love" (Eph 4:15).

Assume that Most of Your Community are Not Intuitive: Research on personality typology indicates that 75% of the population collects information through their five senses—seeing, smelling, touching, hearing and tasting. In other words, most people cannot read the minds of Jesus house leaders; they need Jesus' priorities clearly spelled out. That being the case, I never assumed that relational values would be caught apart from them being written down, periodically taught up front and passed along via heart discipleship.

Connect Relational Values into the Community's On-Ramping Process: Effectively assimilating new participants into a Jesus house is a dynamic process that evolves with its size. At the same time, whatever the strategy, it is essential that a focused effort be made to impart the primacy of God's love and the related, affirmed values.

Keep Advocating for Discipleship that Apprentices: Paul instructed Timothy to replicate his process: *"The things you have heard me say in the presence of many witnesses, entrust to reliable men who will teach others also" (2 Tim 2:2).* While each leadership segment benefits from upfront messaging, the most important relationally-focused discipleship strategy is always life-on-life mentoring that includes praying, teaching and showing.

A Follow Up Letter about Alignment

"To the angel of the church in Ephesus write:

These are the words of him who holds the seven stars in his right hand and walks among the seven golden lampstands. I know your deeds, your hard work and your perseverance. I know that you cannot tolerate wicked people, that you have tested those who claim to be apostles but are not, and have found them false. You have persevered and have endured hardships for my name, and have not grown weary.

Yet I hold this against you: You have forsaken the love you had at first. Consider how far you have fallen! **Repent and do the things you did at first.** *If you do not repent, I will come to you and remove your lampstand from its place. But you have this in your favor: You hate the practices of the Nicolaitans, which I also hate.*

Whoever has ears, let them hear what the Spirit says to the churches. To the one who is victorious, I will give the right to eat from the tree of life, which is in the paradise of God.   Rev. 2:1-7

This chapter started with the word *patience* and my convictions about it.

Patiently aligning the many hearts of a community to God's relational thoughts and ways is so challenging. It seems so slow on a daily basis, but over time, transformation is stunning if leadership is persistent and stays the course.

The early chapters of Revelation provide us with great insights about this very challenge. Seven letters from Jesus to various congregations in Asia are detailed in chapters two and three, and serve as a rich resource for better understanding the difficulty of sustaining Jesus-aligned houses.

Did you note the stern warning Jesus issued to the Ephesians that I bolded in the above quotation? Apparently, this church's leaders were failing to keep Jesus as the cornerstone as Paul had taught and modeled for them.

If Jesus were to write your community a letter today, what would He say?

Aligning a Culture to Love

Equipping Strategies

Intimacy with God is the starting point for realigning a culture to love

Helping disciples learn and obey God's Word accelerates alignment towards Jesus' values

Walking the teaching talk accelerates culture shifts towards love

Jesus' relational values become daily norms as godly value-carriers are prayed for, taught, apprenticed and selected

Empowering Strategies

Walk the Talk in Depth with the 3

Model to the 3 as You Invest in the 9

Position the 9 to Influence the 70

Equip the 70 to Influence the 420

Section One:
Relational Value Statement

Source: Antioch New England

Relational Values

The people of Antioch New England affirm our complete devotion to the Father's and Jesus' heart for people as expressed by these values.

Passionate Worship
Loving Jesus extravagantly

Jesus said that the Father is seeking those who worship Him in Spirit and in truth. We practice a life of worship that invites the presence of Jesus into all that we say and do. *See also Mt. 26:6-13; Jn. 4:23, 5:19-23, 14:21, 15:15; Col. 3:16, 17*

Humble Service
Looking beyond ourselves

Jesus came to serve, not to be served. He modeled this selfless lifestyle with both His disciples as well as society's lost, outcast, and oppressed. As Jesus' disciples, we follow Jesus' example and prioritize the needs of others. *See also Is. 53:1-12; Mt. 15:34-39, 20:25-28; Jn. 13:1-17; Eph. 4:1-3; Phil. 2:1-11*

Authentic Relationships
Cultivating a community of trust

Jesus' relationships were marked by honesty, vulnerability, and accountability. We aspire to be genuine and gracious with those inside and outside the church. In doing so, we demonstrate our unwavering commitment to one another. *See also Mt. 18:15-17; Acts 2:42-47; Rom. 15:5-7; Eph. 4:15; Col. 3:12-15*

Honoring Collaboration
Empowering the strengths of others

Jesus lived with and developed an exceptional team of disciple-makers. Their diverse spiritual gifts, talents, and personalities joined together to become the epicenter of the new Church—the hope of the world. As Jesus' followers, we emulate His process by honoring and empowering the unique grace that resides within every believer. *See also Eccl. 4:9-12; Rom. 12:3-8; 1 Cor. 12; Heb. 10:24-25; 1 Pt. 4:10; Rev. 5:9*

Courageous Generosity
Excelling in the joy of giving

Jesus modeled selfless generosity. After Pentecost, His disciples followed His lead as they shared resources with one another. His extravagant love continues to inspire us to work diligently, live simply, and give joyfully. *See also Mt. 25:14-30, 26:6-13; Acts 2:44-45, 4:32-35; Rom. 12:13; 2 Cor. 8-9; Jas. 2:14-19*

Radical Compassion
Engaging brokenness with the heart of Jesus

Jesus looked at broken humanity through the lens of love and responded with compassion. He loved everyone just as they needed to be loved. We follow Jesus' lead by seeing the world through God's grace-filled eyes, and becoming real-time messengers of His grace, hope, and healing. *See also Ex. 22:21-25; Ps. 146; Is. 58, 61; Mt. 9:35-38, 25:31-46; Lk. 7:22-23; Eph. 4:32; Jas. 1:26-27*

Section One:
Relational Case Study

Author: Bill Jacobs

Bill Jacobs is one of the dear ministry colleagues I mentioned in the Chapter Five. I met him as a member of a larger community (the "five-hundred") I was serving and based on his character and capacity, I invited him to be a "seventy" level leader. His positive impact on that team led me to pursue him as a staff member and eventually, he emerged as a "core influencer" within the church's staff.

I am grateful that he has written this case study as it relates to relational values and I hope you find it helpful. It's a strong example of what I have been seeking to communicate in Section One.

Covenant Church in Winterville, NC was chartered as a United Methodist Church in 1993. By 2002, the church had grown and so had the staff. Weekly attendance exceeded 1,000 per weekend and there were about a dozen people on staff.

Charlie joined the staff as Executive Director in 2002 in the midst of a congregational crisis and related staff transitions. In partnership with the new Lead Pastor (David Brownlee), he initiated two separate, but parallel strategies. The first was focused on building godly unity among the staff by catalyzing them to articulate the Kingdom ideals that would define their ministry together. This 9-month process was spearheaded by a handful of staff and is detailed below.

The second strategy was to involve the larger church in a process of clarifying its Kingdom identity (DNA) – specifically its mission, values, beliefs and vision. It was also led by a team and our objective was to be guided and informed by the witness of the New Testament. This two-year, highly participative learning process enabled the congregation and its leadership to discern, affirm, document and communicate a God-honoring vision with Jesus as the foundational cornerstone.

A Key Process Assumption

As these two strategies began, a new approach to decision-making was modeled through Charlie and David's leadership, namely discernment and consensus.

Today, this style of ministry together has become an established pattern for Covenant's leadership teams. We strive to discern God's will rather than make decisions. We prayerfully listen and study the Bible for God's input as to how to walk out our vision, mission, values and beliefs. What is His best, how do we communicate it and align our lives to make it happen?

Consensus is the process we use for discernment. We pray for God to guide us in forming our teams and for the work they will do. Once established, they continue to pray over their focus and related action steps. We believe that, as at the Jerusalem Council (Acts 15), if something seems good to everyone on the team, it seems good to the Spirit. We do not vote. If one person cannot live with a decision and has another option to offer, we keep talking until unity emerges.

For our staff, discernment and consensus have been and continue to be keys to our staff's effectiveness. We have found they offer us two essential realities: 1) the best chance of overcoming the weeds of electioneering votes to get our way that is so common within our American, democratic culture and 2) a greater capacity to follow God's will in a unified and committed way.

Discerning Staff Values

Leading the Team-Based Church by George Cladis was a catalytic resource for the staff team to discern its workplace values. Having read this book and been coached by Charlie, these staff leaders served as pacesetters.

Together, the existing staff began to pray and read Scripture in order to clarify how Jesus wanted them to work together. They wrote down all the related biblical values they discovered, and began a process of grouping and prioritizing them. (This same process would soon be utilized on a broader scale within the congregation.) After several months, the staff leaders presented their colleagues with a first draft with the following four values: Teamwork; Trust; Respect; Communication.

In time, all staff members (and our lay leadership personnel team) agreed by consensus to these values and received individual copies of the summary document to display in their workspaces. A poster-sized, parchment copy was signed by all employees at a staff chapel and displayed in our main office entrance. As new employees joined staff, they also signed the original and received an individual copy.

About a year after these shared values were in place, the staff realized there should be another value added: Excellence. Once consensus was reached, this new value was added.

For several years, we spent a few staff meetings annually to review the staff values and assess how we were doing in living them out and whether they were still valid and sufficient.

After Charlie's transition off staff and about 8 years after the values were put in place, representative teammates from each area of staff spent several months reviewing the values and proposed a revised set of values (see 2011 version below). The team again reviewed with our lay leadership personnel team and the staff agreed by consensus to the revised edition. The values now are: Glorifying God; Integrity; Truth and Grace; Teamwork; and Discipleship

Embedding the Values

Once the staff values were initially affirmed in 2003, they remained an ongoing focal point. Periodically, staff meetings included a time to affirm those who were excelling at modeling one of the values. Staffers were also encouraged to write notes of affirmation to other staffers who exhibited them in their work. Occasionally, Charlie elicited input and would recognize exemplary contributors with a trophy for each value. These trophies were reengineered from old softball trophies church teams had won in the past. Two that stood out were an old school telephone headset for the *Communication* trophy and an Aretha Franklin CD cover of "RESPECT" for that value.

In addition to the fact that there were trophy winners, every staff member received several notes of affirmation in the process. There were no losers! And the stories of victorious value living not only affirmed each individual, but also inspired the team as a whole. I recall visiting the office one day (I was not on staff at the time) and borrowing a trophy to share in training I was doing with another organization. The receptionist volunteered to show me the notes she had received during the most recent ceremony. She was as proud of the notes as if they were trophies!

Once established, the Staff Values became a part of a prospective employee's interview process as well as their initial orientation if hired. The values were also added to every job description and staff evaluations specifically addressed these "Shared Responsibilities." (They followed Primary and Secondary Responsibilities that outlined a staffer's distinctive contributions.)

To this day, the values continue to be displayed in our main office and conference room. They are in the personnel handbook each employee receives and a specified part of each team member's performance evaluation.

Insights/Lessons Learned

Multiple principles have been learned and reinforced through this process.

- Wide-spread and genuine participation is critical in order for people to take ownership of the values. People must engage with the ideas and seek to clarify understanding if people are going to live by them.

- Conflict often reveals the importance and benefit of having clearly stated Staff Values. When interpersonal conflict arises within our staff, the first thing we do is examine whether there is a value being violated. Most of the time, we discover that at least one value is a part of the conflict. The conversations can then begin with how we have each agreed to work together and how a particular value has not been modeled. While this does not make the conversation easy, it is extremely helpful to begin from a point of how we have agreed to do ministry together.

- The values must be kept alive. Find ways to display them and create conversations about them.

- Modeling and accountability are essential ingredients to the ongoing existence of these values. Walk the talk and expect others to as well.

- Initiate periodic all staff reviews of the values in order to assess how the team is doing at living them out. Determine whether issues have arisen that indicate the values need revision. Is there a value missing that any recurring conflicts might suggest? Does the language need updating? Do any values need additional clarification?

Final Thoughts

Discerning the Kingdom values that define how servants partner together is an excellent team-building strategy. It serves to both accelerate everyone's commitment to Jesus and His Church as well as build unity of purpose.

> *"The body is a unit, though it is made up of many parts; and though all its parts are many, they form one body. So it is with Christ." "So that there should be no division in the body, but that its parts should have equal concern for each other. If one part suffers, every part suffers with it; if one part is honored, every part rejoices with it."* 1 Corinthians 12:12, 25-26

The staff of Covenant United Methodist Church, in partnership with one another, has discerned these values to guide our collective journey of faith. By the Grace of God, we aspire to live by these values in all that we do.

Staff Values - 2011

As a staff member of Covenant Church, I commit to loving my colleagues well. I will be exhibiting this by the way I live into and hold others accountable to these values we have deemed to be of the utmost importance.

Glorifying God - *"This is to my Father's glory, that you bear much fruit, showing yourselves to be my disciples." John 15:8*

Embraces:
- Submitting daily my will for His will
- Living a worshipful lifestyle
- Having a faithful prayer life
- Being faithful, fruitful, fulfilled, and making God famous
- Hearing God say "Well Done"

Integrity - *"So I strive always to keep my conscience clear before God and man." Acts 24:16*

Embraces:
- Being truthful and authentic in all situations
- Honoring my commitments
- Aligning my actions with God's principles

Team Ministry - *"Two are better than one, because they have a good return for their work: If one falls down, his friend can help him up. But pity the man who falls and has no one to help him up." Ecclesiastes 4:9-10*

Embraces:
- Responding to the leading of the Holy Spirit
- Communicating clearly throughout ALL ministries
- Working together in unity to fulfill the mission of a common purpose
- Being mindful and considerate of others' workloads
- Valuing others' gifts, strengths and passions
- Trusting and respecting the opinions, input, and perspectives of others

Truth & Grace - *"The Word became flesh and made his dwelling among us. We have seen his glory, the glory of the one and only Son, who came from the Father, full of grace and truth." John 1:14*

Embraces:
- Extending grace and forgiveness in order to promote healthy relationships
- Speaking the truth in love

Discipleship - *"And the things you have heard me say in the presence of many witnesses entrust to reliable people who will also be qualified to teach others." 2 Timothy 2:2*

Embraces:

- Intentionally following Jesus while bringing others along
- Committing to being discipled and to discipling others
- Abiding with Christ through the practice of Spiritual Disciplines

Bill and his family joined Covenant Church in 1997 after moving to Greenville, NC earlier that year. He served as a small group leader, was on the "Soil Prep Team" that helped discern the congregation's values, the church's personnel team, and the building steering team as we designed the churches' newest facility.

In 2007, he joined the Covenant staff, leading support areas of administration, human resources and facilities, and serving on the executive leadership team. He celebrated 10 years on the staff in 2017.

He is a Certified Lay Speaker in the United Methodist Church and earned his BA Degree from the University of South Carolina and his MBA from East Carolina University. He is a Certified Senior Professional in Human Resources and a Certified Professional in Supply Management.

Section One:
Relational Culture Survey

Walking out Jesus' culture of love is realized through an ongoing process of realignment to His relational values. Accordingly, He calls us into a transformational process: *"If anyone would come after me, let them deny themselves, pick up their cross and follow Me" (Mk 8:35).*

With this in mind, identifying the gaps between Jesus' values and our reality through focused feedback is valuable. When specific areas of growth are clarified, disciples will be able to more clearly see relational strongholds and identify the relevant truths and strategies that will accelerate godliness.

What follows is an example of an assessment tool—a *relational culture survey*. This sample is based on the relational values highlighted in Ephesians 4, and can be used to assess a person, a team and/or a whole community. If your community has already established and affirmed its own relational ideals, simply adapt this template to fit your language.

Relational Culture Survey Template

Instructions: This instrument is designed to be a **confidential exercise** that assesses the relational behavior of a predetermined "subject"—a person, team or larger community.

As you will see, each Ephesians 4 facet of love is represented by three (3) related dysfunctional behaviors. Those completing the assessment are asked to use a 4-point scale to rate how often they observe the "subject" modeling this behavior. (If the "subject" is more than one person – i. e. "*members of the leadership team*" -- answers should reflect the entire group being assessed.) Evaluators should trust their gut and respond with their first impressions.

The 4-Point Scale:

1 Very Common	2 Frequently	3 Infrequently	4 Almost Never

Humility

vs. 4:2 "Be completely humble"

...a modest view of one's own importance

How often do you experience the subject.......?

1. Emphasizing their own agenda and interests? _____
2. Ignoring or disregarding others? _____
3. Recounting their accomplishments in order to be noticed? _____

> ## The *Relational Culture Survey* in its entirety
> ## is now available at HouseofJesus.net

Section Two

Catalyzing a Jesus-aligned, Equipping Culture

Key Passages: Lk 10; Eph 4:11-16; 1 Pt 4:10; 1 Cor 12, 14; Rom 12:4-8

With the pre-eminent values of sacrificial love now in place, the next right step to align your culture to Jesus is to embrace the Father's values for equipping disciples for Kingdom service. In the following chapters, we will review how the Father and Jesus prepare Their people for anointed service (Chapter Six), unpack how to establish these equipping values within a Jesus house (Chapter Seven), and learn how to drive this culture of equipping within a structure that effectively empowers leaders (Chapter Eight). Like the last section, this one will also conclude with a Case Study that exemplifies the Father's values in action, a related Culture Survey for assessing current norms and an example of affirmed equipping values.

Chapter Six

The Father's Equipping Values

Don't you believe that I am in the Father, and that the Father is in me? The words I say to you I do not speak on my own authority. Rather, it is the Father, living in me, who is doing his work.   JOHN 14:10

Twenty plus years ago, I was working diligently to articulate a user-friendly language for biblical training strategies, what I now call equipping-based empowerment. I had discovered Jethro, and his insights on training and decentralized leadership. I was constantly rereading the Gospels and the rest of the New Testament exploring Jesus' and Paul's strategies for mentoring and mobilizing disciples into ministry. Additionally, I was devouring whatever relevant books, recordings and conferences I could find on related subjects such as spiritual gifts, Kingdom leadership and apprenticing.

Then I met Don Cousins and Bruce Bugbee.

After attending their conference on equipping-based churches, I abandoned my "from scratch" recipe and embraced their template. When I returned home, their notebook did not go on my shelf; it went on my desk – right in the middle. Doubt me?

Watch their testimonial videos related to their current *Leadershift Series* published by Shift Press.[1] That's what I looked like when I had more hair!

Though this chapter and section are grounded in what I have learned in the Word and years of equipping leaders in ministry, Don and Bruce's fingerprints are all over these pages. I will always be grateful for their investment in me and truth be told, this book is essentially another implementation guide for their philosophy of equipping.

Equipping Values in the Flesh

As I highlighted in Chapter Three, my first introduction to the Father's love was through Jesus. The same is true as it relates to equipping others for ministry. The Father knew it would be easier for me and many others to understand His culture of training and ministry placement through observing Jesus. And that is exactly what happened. As I kept reading through the New Testament, this truth was confirmed: *Jesus' lifestyle of equipping and empowering His followers was sourced in His Dad!*

> *Don't you believe that I am in the Father, and that the Father is in me? The words I say to you I do not speak on my own authority. Rather, it is the Father, living in me, who is doing his work.* John 14:10

> *The Son is the radiance of God's glory and the exact representation of his being, sustaining all things by his powerful word. Heb 1:3a*

The balance of this chapter is a broad, brush-stroke summary of what I now see about equipping when I open God's Word, read the lines and between them as well. This summary will provide a picture of what it would look like for Jesus house leaders to discern and affirm His leadership ways.

---

[1] Don and Bruce's *Leadershift* resources are a gold mine that combines both biblical insights, real life experiences and practical principles. I have learned so much from each of them and encourage you to do the same.

Equipping Value #1: Compelling Clarity

The LORD Almighty has sworn, "Surely, as I have planned, so it will be, and as I have purposed, so it will happen. Is 14:24

I make known the end from the beginning, from ancient times, what is still to come. I say, 'My purpose will stand, and I will do all that I please.' From the east I summon a bird of prey; from a far-off land, a man to fulfill my purpose. What I have said, that I will bring about; what I have planned, that I will do. Is 46:10-11

But the plans of the LORD stand firm forever, the purposes of his heart through all generations.   *Ps 33:11*

His intent was that now, through the church, the manifold wisdom of God should be made known to the rulers and authorities in the heavenly realms, according to his eternal purpose that he accomplished in Christ Jesus our Lord.   *Eph 3:10-11*

See also Jer 29:11; Eph 1:11; Rev 7:9ff, 21.

I love my four grandchildren Bennett, Zach, Jackson and Mac. They are so cute and say the funniest things. I am sure they will grow up to be wise, Kingdom disciples, but right now, I delight in their naïve view of the world.

I am sure my Father in heaven feels the same about me. For so long, I had this naïve notion that the creation story (Gen 1-2) was God's first action step to realize His plan for our world. How mistaken I was!

I Peter 1:20 provides us with an amazing insight: *"He (Jesus) was chosen before the creation of the world, but was only revealed in these last times for your sake."*

Wow! Before the existence of our planet, the Father was already at work on achieving His eternal plan for the redemption of all who place their hope and trust in Him (Ps 147:11).

I now understand that the Father's clarity regarding a New Jerusalem (Rev 21) and what it would cost Him predates earth's existence. This loving, redemptive destination has always been in His head and heart—the Father started with this clear "win" in mind!

The fact of the matter is that as image bearers of God, we plan the very same way all the time. Don't believe me? I'll prove it!

Assume that at this moment, for whatever reason, it would be a win for you to buy some bread. Now imagine where you are going to go to get it. Since you have decided where, I want you to determine the optimal route you are going to take to arrive at that destination.

Do you realize how you determined the best and most efficient route?

You very quickly figured out how to get from the store with bread to your current location and then reversed the sequence. It's how GPS works. It starts with the destination and subsequently calculates the path that will be needed to get there from where you are.

This is known as "reverse engineering" and it is everywhere. We design buildings then figure out the sequence and steps necessary to make it happen. We imagine meals and then gather what is needed including a recipe. We decide what we are going to wear today and go find those items. Life is a constant process of gaining clarity regarding our preferred future and then following a reverse engineered path to achieve it.

God's equipping of His children is the same way as we can see in Eph 2:10!

For we are God's handiwork, created in Christ Jesus to do good works, which God prepared in advance for us to do.   *Eph 2:10*

The Father's way of achieving His intricate plans is amazing! He is fully aware of the people ("good work") that He desires for us to serve in the future ("in advance"). And based on their needs, He equips, trains and develops our heart and hands ("God's handiwork" and "prepared") so that our character and capacities are readied for these opportunities.

Do you see the great clarity of His multi-level plan? He accomplishes the wins He desires for us (walking out His handiwork) as well as the wins He desires for those He has called us to serve (their needs being met). Boom![2]

The Father starts with the "wins" in mind

Clarity makes....
uniqueness undeniable
direction unquestionable
enthusiasm transferable
work meaningful
synergy possible
success definable
focus sustainable
leadership credible
uncertainty approachable

An excerpt from **Church Unique** by Will Mancini

Equipping Value #2: Anointed Fit

But select capable men from all the people—men who fear God, trustworthy men who hate dishonest gain—and appoint them as officials over thousands, hundreds, fifties and tens.   Ex 18:21

And David shepherded them with integrity of heart; with skillful hands he led them.   Ps 78:72

One of those days Jesus went out to a mountainside to pray, and spent the night praying to God. When morning came, he called his disciples to him and chose twelve of them, whom he also designated apostles;   Lk 6:12-13

---

[2]   Steve Addison's book *What Jesus Started* affirms the same: our Lord's ministry began with clarity about the end game of taking the Gospel to the ends of the earth. He unpacks this in Chapter One – Why Jesus Came.

Brothers and sisters, choose seven men from among you who are known to be full of the Spirit and wisdom. We will turn this responsibility over to them   *Acts 6:3*

Each of you should use whatever gift you have received to serve others, as faithful stewards of God's grace in its various forms.

1 Pt 4:10

See also Jer 29:11; Eph 2:10, 4:16; 2 Tim 2:2

Once the Father has spoken His clear, preferred future, He calls the disciples who fit His plan – servants with the right character (heart) and capacity (spiritual gifts, experience, personality etc.) to make it happen.[3]

We just saw this reality in 1 Peter 1:20. God the Father omnisciently knew there would be a barrier to His Revelation 21 vision of unhindered fellowship with His children, namely Sin. This heavenly vision would need to overcome this problem of Sin with a perfect sacrifice. Accordingly, He identified and called the only person who fits this criterion, His Son Jesus.

There are many other examples of the Father securing just the right person for His plans as we see can see in the sampling of texts just listed:

1)   The Father secures the right person, Moses, to lead Israel from Egypt to the Promised Land. In time and with Jethro's coaching, Moses does the same thing by securing the right leaders with proven character and capacity to lead 1,000s, 100s, 50s and 10s.

2)   The Father chooses the perfect king for Israel, David. This young man's heart (character) and skill (capacity) are perfect for God's plan for His people.

---

[3]   I do recognize that Saul (Paul) is an exception to the pattern we see throughout the Bible.

3) After a season of intentional relationship building, Jesus prayerfully selects the right twelve to be strategic leaders in His new movement.

4) In Acts, we see God inspiring Jerusalem leaders to decentralize their leadership functions and create a focused team to address unmet needs in the community. Accordingly, they initiate a process to invite and affirm seven additional servants to help out. Stephen, Philip and the five others subsequently prove themselves to be the right people for this new role.

These examples serve to reinforce Ephesians 2:10 and confirm that there is a right place in ministry for all the Father's children! He faithfully prepares us and related opportunities that advance His Kingdom.

The Father invites the right people into the right roles

Equipping Value #3: Patient Apprenticing

The LORD had said to Abram, "Go from your country, your people and your father's household to the land I will show you. "I will make you into a great nation, and I will bless you; I will make your name great, and you will be a blessing. I will bless those who bless you, and whoever curses you I will curse; and all peoples on earth will be blessed through you." So Abram went, as the LORD had told him.   *Gen 12:1-4*

Then the LORD said, "Rise and anoint him; this is the one." So Samuel took the horn of oil and anointed him in the presence of his brothers, and from that day on the Spirit of the LORD came powerfully upon David. Samuel then went to Ramah.

      1 Samuel 16:12-13

Jesus called his twelve disciples to him and gave them authority to drive out impure spirits and to heal every disease and sickness… These twelve Jesus sent out with the following instructions: "Do not go among the Gentiles or enter any town of the Samaritans. Go rather to the lost sheep of Israel. Mt 10:1, 5-6

I want you to know, brothers and sisters, that the gospel I preached is not of human origin. I did not receive it from any man, nor was I taught it; rather, I received it by revelation from Jesus Christ. Gal 1:11-12

See also Acts 9:27; Phil 4:9; 2 Tim 2:2

I huddled with two amazing disciples recently, Sam and Justin. They are currently part of my orbit and I had the great privilege of sharing with them a few things I have learned over the years.

Towards the end of my "sermon," I paused and reminded them that God had been preparing me for our appointment for forty-six years—the current span of my journey with Jesus. I'm not sure they really grasped the truthfulness of that statement, but it was spot on. Some of what I shared that day were insights from my earliest months as a disciple while others were fresh from the prior week.

Here's the point: Not only does God prepare good works in advance for us to do (investing in people like Sam and Justin), He prepares us in advance (equipping me to be ready to serve my brothers)! We were His workmanship in our mother's womb (Ps 130). We are His workmanship as His redeemed children (Col 1:13-14). We are His workmanship through the sanctifying work of His Spirit – the One who makes us holy (Phil 3:12-14). The Father excels at patiently apprenticing His saints for the work of ministry![4]

As you reflect on this value, it's important to remember that apprenticing (or mentoring) is a multi-step process that involves the following:

---

[4] Please read Chapters 3 and 4 from Dave and Jon Ferguson's book *Exponential*. It's great stuff on how we can do the same by apprenticing other disciples.

I watch you (my mentor) do it;
We do it together;
You watch me do it;
I do it on my own.

This was Jesus' preferred teaching strategy for preparing His followers for Kingdom service. He equipped them to do ministry through their: 1) watching *(observing Him talking with outcasts)*; 2) partnering *(helping Him feed 5,000 with a few loaves and fishes)*; 3) practicing *(being sent out to surrounding communities to preach)* and; 4) leadership of others *(Jesus' commissioning the Apostles and the aftermath of Pentecost)*.

The passages noted above provide additional examples of this kind of patient apprenticing:

1)   God promises Abram that he will experience amazing things in his life (Gen 12), but they are not fully realized for fifty or so years (Gen 22). Abram needs a lot of equipping to fully step into God's destiny for him.

2)   David also needs lots of training as well. Having already learned many lessons about God's faithfulness, David is anointed by Samuel (1 Samuel 16), but does not become king for eight or so more years (2 Samuel 2). David has more lessons he needs to learn from the Father.

3)   Jesus supernaturally calls a very broken person, Saul, to minister to the Gentiles (Acts 9), but it takes twelve or so years for Paul to be sent out from Antioch (Acts 13). And as Paul details, Jesus is right in the middle of this preparatory process.

As you can see and probably know already, apprenticing disciples is not just about information, but formation. If information is all you need to be equipped, I can just hand you a clear vision along with related expectations and goals. You now have everything you need and I'm done! But in Jesus' house, this is wishful thinking and it is not the way of the Master.

Jesus-aligned apprenticing is all about transformation. It's a *heart* discipleship process that enables us to increasingly receive God's unsearchable love and then love others accordingly. It's also a *ministry* discipleship process that enables us to discover our unique gifting over time and fully learn to serve others for God's glory.

So why does the Father's (and our) apprenticing need to be patient? Because of disciples like me!

At twenty-three, I had only known Jesus for six years. I understood so little about His thoughts and ways, and was challenged by the most basic ministry assignments.

At thirty-three, my character and capacity had grown quite a bit, but it's painful to remember some of the choices I made in that season. I was still a youngster in the Lord.

At forty-three, my understanding of the breadth and depth of the Father's love was expanding, but I still battled long-standing lies from my childhood. I was also growing in my ministry capacity, but there were still many lessons I had not yet learned.

You might think that at fifty-three – thirty-six years of following Jesus – that the rate of my spiritual growth would have plateaued, but that was not my experience. In fact, in that season, I found myself experiencing a personal revival.

At sixty-three, I am now walking in more freedom and confidence than ever before (Eph 3:12), but I know He has more for me! Over forty-six years and through His grace, I have transitioned from an outsider to the Father's thoughts and ways to become an empowered insider called to serve others with His gospel of Hope.

The Father patiently equips "outsiders" to be "insiders" to His plans[5]

---

[5] Saul is the prototype "outsider"—completely clueless. Over time, however, Paul becomes an "insider" to God's heart and plans. I will be expanding on all these slogans in the next few chapters.

FOR CLARITY: *Apprenticing, mentoring, coaching* and words like them are used in a variety of ways. To avoid confusion, let me clarify what I mean by them.

I am using the words "apprenticing" and "mentoring" to capture the preparation a ministry servant needs to successfully step into a new role or assignment. The focus is onboarding. Excellence in this stage of equipping enables someone to be competent and confident as they begin serving.

"Coaching" is being used to capture what a servant needs to continue thriving in their ministry role. The focus is sustaining. As you can easily imagine, coaching someone so they continue to thrive in ministry almost always involves training them in additional skills and responsibilities which also involves an apprenticing-like process.

Equipping Value #4: Life-giving Coaching

I will counsel you with my loving eye on you.   *Ps 32:8b*

He made known his ways to Moses, His deeds to the people of Israel.   *Ps 103:7*

All this I have spoken while still with you. But the Advocate, the Holy Spirit, whom the Father will send in my name, will teach you all things and will remind you of everything I have said to you.   *John 14:25-26*

See also Ex 18:19ff; Luke 10:1-12; Eph 4:11; 1 and 2 Timothy

These next verses were very confusing to me when I first read them.

Don't you believe that I am in the Father, and that the Father is in me? The words I say to you I do not speak on my own authority. Rather, it is the Father, living in me, who is doing his work.

John 14:10

These words you hear are not my own; they belong to the Father who sent me. John 14:24

One of my first impressions of Jesus was that He was the ultimate super-hero: All powerful, all knowing and totally self-reliant. I guess two out of three isn't bad! Even Jesus received the Father's coaching and ongoing support.

And now it is so clear: Jesus depended upon the Father on a daily basis. He did what He saw the Father doing and said what He heard the Father say. The undergirding of the Father's hand and His Spirit's power is especially visible during Jesus' final days leading up to Calvary. How else could you explain His resilience during His final week as a human?

Jesus also models this value with the Twelve: He patiently apprenticed His team and then provided them with an Additional Coach—the Holy Spirit—to sustain what He had begun.

All this I have spoken while still with you. But the Advocate, the Holy Spirit, whom the Father will send in my name, will teach you all things and will remind you of everything I have said to you. John 14:25-26

The Holy Spirit fully steps into His role after Jesus' ascension and the real fun begins!

The other biblical passages listed above provides additional examples of the importance of an ongoing investment in ministry servants:

1) David, the man after God's heart, receives life-giving coaching from the Father: the essential insights, instruction,

guidance and oversight he needs to persevere as a leader. His Father is always faithful.

2) Moses is repeatedly sustained through his intimate relationship with and the guidance of his heavenly Father. God is smitten with Moses' heart and faithfulness and reveals Himself in supernatural ways so that Moses can endure through tough times.

I would be remiss if I did not confess how much I have struggled with coaching. When I take the time and energy to complete the first three aspects of apprenticing you (letting you watch me, partnering with you and then observing you serve and providing feedback), I am very tempted to move on without ongoing coaching. I am confident you are fully prepared and don't need me anymore.

But here is the reality: If I now expect more from you than I am willing to invest in you, it's just a matter of time before you experience burnout. This is not of God; it is not His way.

The Father always puts more into His people than He takes out

By now, I trust you are beginning to put the pieces of the equipping puzzle together. The Father's selfless love is primary and the starting point for the culture of Jesus' house (Section One). It's the impetus, motivation and explanation for everything God does.

With this foundation in place, the Father's equipping values mobilize loving servants to walk out their anointing as they step into His grace-filled plans as we have just seen:

- He starts with clarity about the destination – Kingdom plans are wins for His servants as well as the people He has prepared us to serve;

- He then calls gifted disciples who fit (character and capacity) – He is delighted when the right people get in the right roles;

- He then patiently apprentices people in and for ministry – He makes faithful outsiders insiders to His ways and plans;

- He then provides life-giving coaching in order to sustain His servants – He always puts more into His children than He takes out.

Can you see, feel and taste this Jesus-aligned culture that Paul wanted to explain to everyone – "the oversight of the house (oikonomia)?

A selfless love for people (Eph 4:1-3, 15, 32) together with a passion for equipping and empowering Kingdom servants for godly plans (Eph 4:11-16) — this is a dynamic combination that fuels His message and ultimately changes the world!

But we are not quite done unpacking the Father's ways. Let's look at one more equipping value.

Equipping Value #5: Honoring Transitions

Then Moses climbed Mount Nebo from the plains of Moab to the top of Pisgah across from Jericho. There the LORD showed him the whole land—from Gilead to Dan, all of Naphtali, the territory of Ephraim and Manasseh, all the land of Judah as far as the Mediterranean Sea, the Negev and the whole region from the Valley of Jericho, the City of Palms, as far as Zoar. Then the LORD said to him, "This is the land I promised on oath to Abraham, Isaac and Jacob when I said, 'I will give it to your descendants.' I have let you see it with your eyes, but you will not crossover into it." Deut 34:1-4

When they had crossed, Elijah said to Elisha, "Tell me, what can I do for you before I am taken from you?" "Let me inherit a double portion of your spirit," Elisha replied. "You have asked a difficult thing," Elijah said, "yet if you see me when I am taken from you, it will be yours—otherwise, it will not." 2 Kings 2:9-10

When they had finished eating, Jesus said to Simon Peter, "Simon son of John, do you love me more than these?" John 21:15

In my former book, Theophilus, I wrote about all that Jesus began to do and to teach until the day he was taken up to heaven, after giving instructions through the Holy Spirit to the apostles he had chosen. After his suffering, he presented himself to them and gave many convincing proofs that he was alive. He appeared to them over a period of forty days and spoke about the kingdom of God. Acts 1:1-3

Instead, speaking the truth in love, we will grow to become in every respect the mature body of him who is the head, that is, Christ. Eph 4:15

For we are God's handiwork, created in Christ Jesus to do good works, which God prepared in advance for us to do. Eph 2:10

As I have just highlighted, these equipping values are sequential. Until you have clarity about the desired "wins," it's hard to know which people fit the needed ministry roles. And until the right people are apprenticed, it's unlikely that servants can step into their roles with competence and confidence. And if there is not ongoing support for these disciples, they will rarely thrive and fulfill their calling.

But even if you emulate these first four values with excellence, it's only a matter of time before ministry servants move in a new direction. Kingdom servants transitioning out of ministry roles is unavoidable and typically occurs due to one of four, common reasons.

1)   God is calling this disciple into a new and different "good work";

2)   The servant is not a good fit for their current role;

3)   The servant has not been adequately trained for their current role; [6]

4)   They have disqualified themselves by making a poor choice.

On multiple occasions, I have personally experienced the first two kinds of transitions.

Example of #1: There was a time when I loved and was fully called to do ministry with secondary students. It was a daily joy and I remember those days fondly. I loved my "kids" and have many great stories that I could share. But one day, I began to realize that God's call on life was in transition. No one had offended me. I had not failed in my service to the kids. And yet, the original passion God had given me was clearly shifting and a new burden was beginning to emerge. Over the next season, I took my next right step of faith as I responded to God's new plans.

Example of #2: I have also been the wrong person in a role; the second common reason for many ministry transitions. Interestingly, it was not that way at first. On one occasion, I had thrived for seven years in that place of ministry, but two things changed. The church's needs changed and I changed as well. At the time, it was not easy to acknowledge my lack of fit, but deep down, I knew what needed to happen. Before long, I initiated a process of securing a successor.

In both cases, the Father honored my gifting, relationships and heart along the way. He taught me new lessons and skills that set the stage for emerging opportunities He had prepared in advance me and others. He brought trusted people into my life who could reinforce His wisdom with love. He opened new doors to challenge me. Most of all, He gave me new passion for my next steps of faith.

My experience with an honoring Father is nothing new as the texts above reveal:

---

[6] We will be coming back to #2 and 3. As you can see, these failures reflect the equipping leader's decisions and actions. Transitions under my leadership have always triggered times of deep reflections: What do I need to own? What do I need to learn from this experience?

1) The Father honored His friend Moses with a glimpse of the long-term goal for which God had spoken about for years;

2) The Father honored both Elijah's transition out of his prophetic role while simultaneously confirming Elisha in his new role;

3) The Father guided Jesus through a four-week transitional process (see the end of each Gospel) that would help His 3, 12, 70 and 500 leadership community to embrace an "ends of the earth" vision (Acts 1:8);

4) Jesus honors Peter by lovingly restoring him after a painful lapse as a leader.

Truth be told, no two transitions are identical.

At times, they are filled with affirmation, a sense of accomplishment and celebrations. Even when a challenging geographic move is being triggered, Kingdom servants walking into their Father's new plans is always a good thing.

But sometimes, transitions cut to the bone. It can hurt deeply when you no longer fit in a ministry role in which you once excelled. And it is especially painful for servants that have made poor choices and disqualified themselves not to mention others in their orbit who feel it deeply as well.

Thank goodness the Father and His plans keep us on track if we are willing to follow!

Our Father lovingly guides our next, right steps of faith

The Apostle's Teaching

Apostle Paul also provides a level of written clarity about equipping God's people unlike any other biblical author:

"So Christ Himself gave the apostles, the prophets, the evangelists, the pastors and teachers, to equip his people for works of service, so that the body of Christ may be built up until we all reach unity in the faith and in the knowledge of the Son of God and become mature, attaining to the whole measure of the fullness of Christ. Then we will no longer be infants, tossed back and forth by the waves, and blown here and there by every wind of teaching and by the cunning and craftiness of people in their deceitful scheming. Instead, speaking the truth in love, we will grow to become in every respect the mature body of him who is the head, that is, Christ. From him the whole body, joined and held together by every supporting ligament, grows and builds itself up in love, as each part does its work."   *Eph 4:11-16*

The Apostle reinforces and adds to what we have just learned from observing the Father's and Jesus' ways. What follows are several observations from this passage that will assist us as we transition to the implementation of these five equipping values.

1) *Christ Himself:* This culture of equipping I am emphasizing is a God thing that Jesus modeled. I have certainly benefitted from my readings on leadership and organizational systems from recent secular authors. But for me, what we learn from Jesus' example and God's Word about training, discipleship and empowerment is primary resource for aligning our ways to God.

2) *Gave:* This past tense indicative verb (edothe) reinforces what seems obvious: Jesus envisioned and trained these five spiritual gifts (APEST for short – Apostle, Prophet, Evangelist, Shepherd, Teacher) to function as a unified team.[7] Alan Hirsch

---

[7] Checkout the book of Acts and how the Apostles with their APEST giftings collaborated and led together in Chapters 1 and 6.

and Tim Catchim do a great job of addressing this verb and its meaning their book *The Permanent Revolution* which I highly encourage you to read.[8]

3) Equip: This additional key verb is the Greek word kataristmon whose meaning conveys the notion of setting a broken bone, mending a frayed net, furnishing an empty house, restoring to mint condition or training an athlete. Paul's selection of this term underscores that equipping disciples to serve in ministry is much more about development than delegation. Once someone has completed the equipping process needed for a role, however, empowerment is a vital next step hence my phrase "equipping-based empowerment".

4) The whole body…grows and builds itself up in love as each part does its work: This is Paul's hope and vision for the culture of Jesus' houses: every disciple serving in love and through their supernatural anointing—the kind of culture that fuels His Gospel!

Supernatural Combo

Remember Danny Silk from Chapter Three?

He is the Executive Pastor of Bethel Church and the author of *Culture of Honor: Sustaining a Supernatural Environment.*

Remember what he said about his church's culture?

> *What you might not have heard is that these supernatural events are directly related to the supernatural culture that the community of saints at Bethel have been developing for over a decade.*

Silk's book identifies **two ingredients** within their culture: 1) godly relationships (which I have already referenced) and 2) Ephesians

---

[8]   Chapter One (3-26) from *The Permanent Revolution: Apostolic Imagination and Practice for the 21st Century Church.* Josey-Bass, 2012.

4:11 equipping.[9] From my vantage point, Bethel's leadership has discovered that walking out the Father's values for selfless love and equipping-based empowerment catalyzes a supernatural culture.

Buckle your seatbelt; time to get practical!

---

[9] See Chapter 2 from Silk's *Culture My Honor.* I have recently been reading another book from a Bethel Church staffer, Steve Backlund entitled *Culture of Empowerment: How to Champion People.* It's a good read and worthy of your review. Steve dives deeply into interpersonal and team communication which is essential for creating an equipping-focused community. This and the next few chapters is very much in sync with his fine work.

The Father's Equipping Values

Compelling Clarity
The Father starts with the "wins" in mind

Anointed Fit
The Father invites the right people into
the right roles

Patient Apprenticing
The Father patiently equips "outsiders"
to be "insiders" to His plans

Life-giving Coaching
The Father always puts more into
His people than He takes out

Honoring Transitions
Our Father lovingly guides our next,
right steps of faith

90°

Chapter Seven

Establishing Cornerstone Values of Equipping

> So Christ himself gave the apostles, the prophets, the evangelists, the pastors and teachers, to equip his people for works of service, so that the body of Christ may be built up
>
> EPH 4:11-12

Am I really raising three lawyers?

I don't know if I ever asked that question out loud when my three boys were youngsters, but that's how I felt on numerous occasions. I remember guiding them as they were learning about various responsibilities e. g. house chores, school homework, managing laundry, honoring curfew etc. Having verbally spelled out our household boundaries and then empowering each to live within them, all three would periodically color outside those lines. When I asked them about it, each would often say something like *"But you never told me!"*

Son, are you serious!?

The resulting loss of my hair (and it is mostly gone now) forced me to get smarter and lead better. I started writing down these household boundaries, and had each sign and date them at the appropriate age! By the time they had all left home, multiple "letters of agreement" had been written to document and insure alignment to our family's values.

Once again: In today's sound bite world, the vast majority of people in Jesus' houses benefit from the same kind of written clarity regarding His ways. My life experience is that three-to-five stated, affirmed and transferable values accelerate a house leader's capacity to verbalize and emulate Jesus' passion for equipping-based empowerment (Ex 18). In doing so, it sets the stage for these values to be more easily internalized and then shared within and beyond the community.

This intentional, culture-creating focus is not strategic planning or a decision made and implemented; it is nothing less than a church's deepening agreement with the values of Christ—a gradual transformation of culture. As congregations stay grounded and focused on Christ, they can increasingly understand God's design for the Church and for their own specific fellowship of believers, taking on the blessed role of servants discerning the will of the King. *The Heart of the Matter,* page 95

But there is also a spiritual benefit to a summary of His equipping values and it relates to the schemes of the enemy. Do you remember the Holy Spirit insight that John, Lynn and Sam had as they shared about their struggle to find communities that were aligned to Jesus?

Every Jesus house they had visited these past five years had a common flaw. Each had unknowingly imported one or more values from the surrounding culture, rather than be fully aligned to Him.

Their insight has been my reality. Wherever a Jesus house exists, the enemy infiltrates it with whatever ungodly values have been normalized within the surrounding culture. Satan's strategy is not complicated; here is how the deception works.

Wherever Jesus house participants live, they have, at some level, been socialized into worldly norms through family, schools, workplaces, government and media. The result? They (and me!) unknowingly bring these ungodly behaviors and related lies into

His house with them. Like a computer virus, arrogance, pride, racism, abuse, control, selfishness, sexism, greed, pragmatism and other toxic values enter Jesus' house through us and attempt to take root. Once inside, the enemy does his best to neutralize Jesus' culture of loving relationships and equipping.

The antidote? Consistently stating and affirming Jesus' message and Kingdom values help community leaders to teach and model His priorities, embed them in all equipping leaders, recognize and call out demonic lies, foster life-giving accountability and overcome the enemy.

A Quick Case Study

In Chapter Four, I highlighted a church I served which had discerned and affirmed four relational values as a part of a re-founding process (pg. 64). As a part of the same initiative, they also affirmed two additional values focused on equipping as follows:

Empowering People
A process for equipping and sending Christ's followers
Jesus intentionally modeled, trained and empowered people to be disciple-makers. He has given us His Holy Spirit and commissioned us go to the ends of the earth. Accordingly, all of us as ordinary people are compelled to be prepared and empowered to accomplish a divine mission.

Ministering Together
A strategy for accomplishing God's plan on earth
Jesus commissioned His followers in groups and teams as they went out with His authority to preach, teach, heal and care for those in need. We have been given different gifts and have been designed to work together for the fulfillment of the kingdom of God.

As a senior leader, I loved these values and was deeply committed to them, but they pinched even me at times!

My personality (Myers-Briggs INTJ) and family upbringing make micro-managing and controlling others a comfortable preference, but the Spirit keeps teaching me to lead otherwise. Jesus' culture is not of this world. Biblical clarity regarding His equipping values has, therefore, accelerated my own transformation by helping me to clearly see and walk on His path.

Cornerstone equipping values accelerate alignment to Jesus

Re-Founding Equipping-Based Empowerment

My hope is always that a new Jesus house would affirm and codify His passion for equipping-based empowerment from the outset. But I have never seen or been a part of a community that has done that. As a result, I have helped to re-found these priorities within multiple communities where I have served or consulted. As already stated, this process always begins with articulating and establishing Jesus' relational values. Once in place, doing the same for His values of equipping-based empowerment is step two, but my suggested process strategy for the latter might surprise you.

In Chapter Four, I affirmed a bottoms-up approach as an excellent approach for re-founding Jesus' relational norms within a community. I argued that if lots of participates are involved, the level of buy-in and ownership tend to be much stronger. As it relates to equipping values, however, I typically recommend a top-down approach for the following reasons.

Relevance: Let me use Moses and Jethro's leadership recommendations as an example. Using an estimate of 600,000 Israeli men at the time, Moses will need to ensure that 78,600 or

13% are properly trained to implement the decentralized equipping model his father-in-law has suggested (leaders of 1,000s, 100's, 50's and 10's). Does Moses really need 87% of the men who are not involved in leading to be a part of this restructuring process? Relational values apply to every man, women and child, but equipping values are relevant for a much smaller audience, namely equipping leaders. Accordingly, I suggest a narrower approach.

Complexity: This is another good reason for a top-down approach. I believe the concepts of equipping leadership and spiritual gifts are much more difficult to understand than loving relationships and spiritual fruit. It is easy to find Bible passages that are crystal clear on the nature of godly love. But as we saw in the last chapter, you often have to read between the lines of God's Word to see and understand how the Father and Jesus prepare and mobilize their followers for ministry. My experience: *Non-equipping disciples rarely find the topic of leadership values interesting or helpful.*

Resistance: Did you see this one coming? If a Jesus house has had a Moses-centric model of ministry for any length of time, it can be very difficult to shift to a decentralized, equipping structure.[1] John, Lynn and Sam are fully capable of being equipped to serve others in the name of Christ. But if I have grown accustomed to Moses as my personal shepherd and discipler, I will likely resist their ministry and the notion of equipping-based empowerment. Who wouldn't prefer the leader who has seen a burning bush? Based on my experience, re-founding the values of decentralized equipping is better done with the house's leaders who are fully committed to Jesus' ways.

Leverage equipping leaders to re-found equipping values

---

[1]   You've got to read Don Cousins' book *Experiencing Leadershift: Letting Go of Leadership Heresies.* What a powerful title and book. Moses doing hands on ministry for 600,000 families is methodological heresy! We all need to be like Jesus and invest in 3, 9, 70 etc.

Best Practices for Discerning and Affirming Jesus' Values for Equipping

I frequently joke with Jesus house leaders I meet that I used to be six feet-two inches tall. They can see that I am five-six and so I quickly qualify: *"But I've worked in Jesus' house for 30 plus years and it has chopped me down to size"!*

My bantering has a clear intent and message: *Leading like Jesus is challenging because it involves embracing counter cultural values and ways.* It's totally worth it, but there is a cost.

Here is a handful of truths I have learned about discerning and affirming equipping values as I have advocated for Jesus-aligned houses.

Start by Reaffirming Jesus as the Cornerstone: Remember my four-step process from Chapter One? Unfortunately affirming Jesus' rightful place as the cornerstone is not a one-and-done event for house leaders. As this value-focused process begins, re-engage this truth, dialogue about what it means and recommit to His Lordship. In fact, I'd suggest making it an annual rhythm!

Anticipate the Obstacles: This is somewhat repetitive, but that's OK. From the very outset of this book, I have been highlighting that all too often Jesus' houses mimic the world, rather than being "salt" and "light." In other words, He calls His communities to be counter-cultural, to articulate and model His thoughts and ways, but that is rarely the case. Instead, we tend to allow our houses to be defined by the values of the surrounding culture. If that is true (and I am convinced it is), it's only common sense that this process of discernment might ruffle a few feathers.

In his book *Experiencing Leadershift: Letting Go of Leadership Heresies,* Don Cousins makes the same claim and backs it up. He provides an in-depth and comprehensive picture of how today's Jesus house leaders tend towards a consumeristic model of ministry where they "do the work of ministry", rather than "equip the saints". Please read this groundbreaking work!

Bottom-line: Embracing Jesus' equipping values that prioritizes every disciple being in ministry (Eph 4:16) tends to crucify both house leaders and participants. As house leaders, we must humbly step out of the spotlight and train others to excel beyond us. At the same time, we—the members of Jesus' houses—need to reprioritize our lives and time commitments to faithfully walk out our gifting (1 Pt 4:10). Given this spiritual tug-of-war, here are a few suggestions:

- **Mobilize Prayer Warriors:** Ephesians 6:10-18 underscores what to expect if we walk out a Chapter 4:1-16 culture. Yes, the enemy does have "flaming arrows," but so do we. And ours are more powerful than his! So, catalyze the intercessors to undergird the process and hold up the shield of faith.

- **Declare it Upfront:** Even though this is a leadership-focused initiative, the calling to faithfully serve is an essential teaching for everyone in Jesus' houses (i. e. Mt 25). Publicly share the process beforehand plus the heart and Scripture behind it. Leadership accountability is a good thing.

- **Create an Atmosphere of Confession:** The more I have pressed into this biblical theme, the more I have had to deal with my own ego and prior missteps. As this process unfolds, community leaders are encouraged to be transparent at the right time and in the right way as God's Spirit lovingly corrects them. This can be one of the most significant and powerful steps in the whole process.

Embrace Patience as a Vital Ingredient: I began Chapter Three with a focus on the need to be patient when it comes to following Jesus. Please embrace that mindset as you launch this initiative! If your community has had limited clarity regarding Ephesians 4:11-16, discerning and affirming the Father's and Jesus' equipping values will take time. The reason? This process will likely trigger a culture shift and so patience is essential. It's not that I don't like "add water and stir"; it just doesn't work very often.

Begin Refounding Only After Securing Core Leadership Consensus: Just like establishing a process for discerning relational values, don't move forward until all the essential stakeholders within the community understand and are onboard regarding both the desired outcomes of this initiative and related steps.

Use a Sequenced Strategy: As already highlighted, Jesus utilized a tiered and decentralized structure to guide His investment in Kingdom leaders. My experience suggests that using this same framework is the best approach for this process.

- **Begin from the Top:** In my mind, Peter, James and John represent the senior leaders of Jesus' movement, at least initially. Can you see the Master's focused and deft strategy to win their loyalty and buy in? Jesus sets them up for success by making them early insiders to His plans and priorities. In like fashion, I would encourage your community's senior leader(s) to be front and center as equipping values are discerned and affirmed. Without their ownership, this initiative will likely fail.

- **Pulling in the "Other Nine":** The next tier of leadership — the other nine apostles—are very important to this process and at minimum, should have a strong voice in this process.[2] Within a Jesus house, this group could easily include elders, seasoned and influential disciples and or equipping staff members. Like the discerning of relational values, it is best to include those who will serve as primary value carriers.

  Accomplishing this goal of inclusion can be realized through multiple strategies such as: 1) including them in the

---

[2] Having a "voice" in a process means getting to share one's thoughts and feedback on a project. Having a "vote" means you are one of the individuals who will be a part of the project's decision-making strategy. As this re-founding process is designed, its very helpful to define who has a vote and who has a voice up front.

review of biblical passages related to equipping; 2) pulling in several of them to assist in the writing of a draft statement of values; 3) folding them into the refining process of initial drafts; 4) if an outsider is facilitating the process, link the nine to this catalyst and his/her teaching; 5) mobilizing them as group facilitators to the next tier, the "seventy."[3]

- **Securing the "Seventy" (Lk 10) as Early Adopters:** Everett Rogers coined the phrase "early adopters" to describe those who are quicker to embrace innovation and as a result, influence others.[4] I see this paradigm as a helpful way to envision the influence of this next tier of leaders.[5]

  These leaders will likely come from all the influencers who catalyze the community's discipleship and ministry groups. In my experience, not all will be willing to participate, but giving them the opportunity is honoring while being a great strategy to embed Jesus' passion for equipping-based empowerment in them.

Leverage, but Don't Copy Others: The best time to research and review equipping value statements from other Jesus houses is after a first draft has been written. Leaders benefit from seeing how other communities have captured these same truths, but only after they have mined their own gold from God's Word. As my friend Justin says, hearing God's truth from others is milk; discovering it for yourself with the Spirit's help is meat. So true!

Celebrate a Completed Foundation Plan: Remember in Chapter One how I detailed four ongoing steps that are essential for establishing and sustaining a Jesus house foundation?

---

[3] The tiered, forced choice process described in Chapter 5 can also be effectively used with this process.

[4] See *Diffusion of Innovations* by Everett Rogers for great insights on how members of a community have a tiered response to change.

[5] From my perspective, most of the Luke 10 seventy were a part of the 120 disciples mentioned at the end of Acts 1.

#1: Make Jesus the House's Cornerstone

#2: Incarnationally Testify to God's Grace

#3: Catalyze a Jesus-Aligned, Relational Culture

#4: Catalyze a Jesus-Aligned, Equipping Culture

Once these leader-affirmed cornerstone elements have been codified for the community, a worshipful celebration is in order! Check out the Old Testament for some great examples inspired by a loving Father. He totally understands the value of a godly party that focuses on His goodness and accelerates unity as His priorities are affirmed by all![6]

Cornerstone Learning

All truth belongs to God. So, here is a cornerstone-related story from my season in industry as recounted in my first book.[7] It reinforces the benefit of stated values by which we collectively align our lives.

I learned a great deal about the cornerstone principle as general manager and president of a multi-site retail business with 65 employees. At the time of my hiring, this family business had long ago lost alignment to its founder's cornerstone values and was on the brink of bankruptcy. As an outsider, I knew my job was to restore its original culture and corresponding values, and in so doing, its profitability. Along the way, I unexpectedly witnessed one of the premier secular examples of cornerstone alignment.

My cornerstone-in-action experience occurred when an industry vendor invited me to attend a presentation at the

---

[6] Two examples from my past work: 1) I had a set of staff values printed on parchment (see the Relational Case Study) and had everyone sign it. The value statement was then framed and hung in our office and: 2) I had several hundred equipping leaders ink their thumbs and put their thumb print on a large poster detailing our commitment to disciple others. Leaders initialed their thumb print and the poster was hung in a prominent place.

[7] *The Heart of the Matter;* pg. 93.

Ritz-Carlton in Detroit, Michigan. Well, this boy from Texas had never even seen a Ritz-Carlton, and I was pretty impressed. But what really caught my attention was the way I was treated. Within several hours of arriving, I left my room to attend a program meeting held in a first-floor conference room. I proceeded down the elevator, and as I passed through the lobby, one of the concierges called to me: "Good evening Mr. Halley." Well, I was shocked and surprised. Was I in trouble? How did this guy know my name?

Several hours later, I received another jolt as I passed through the lobby on my way back to my room. Another concierge approached me and said, "Good night, Mr. Halley." Thinking, "Okay, this is weird," I thanked him and kept on going. Then, as I neared my room on the third floor, I encountered yet another Ritz-Carlton employee, with the now-predictable, "Sleep well, Mr. Halley."

That did it! I stopped him in his tracks and asked him to explain what was going on. Politely, he coached me on the values, beliefs, vision and mission of Ritz-Carlton hotels. He proudly said, "Our motto is: 'We are Ladies and Gentlemen Serving Ladies and Gentlemen.'" Then, he went on to show me a small pocket tri-fold that detailed the hotel chain's credo, mission, values, and service principles. Calling guests by their names is a top value at the Ritz. I learned that the front desk employees had discreetly taken my picture upon my arrival and passed it around. Color me impressed! Getting the leaders of a large string of hotels to define and publish the organization's values and mission is one thing. Incarnating those values on a day-to-day basis—particularly on the third floor of just one of the many Ritz-Carlton hotels—is a whole other issue.

I still have that tri-fold and continue to share this little story quite often to make a point. What I learned that day and through numerous subsequent experiences is that all organizations—including the local church—benefit from a well-defined and owned cornerstone. And just like the Ritz-Carlton, living out one's articulated cornerstone is an ongoing, never-ending process of alignment.

Ready to learn more about the ongoing sustaining of Jesus' culture of equipping?

Turn the page!

Establishing Cornerstone Values of Equipping

Cornerstone equipping values accelerate alignment to Jesus

Leverage equipping leaders to re-found equipping values

Best Practices

Start by reaffirming Jesus as the Cornerstone

Anticipate the Obstacles

Embrace Patience as a Vital Ingredient

Begin Refounding Only After Securing Core Leadership Consensus

Use a Sequenced Strategy

Leverage, but Don't Copy Others

Celebrate a Completed Foundation Plan

90°

Chapter Eight

Aligning a Culture to Equipping

Not that I have already obtained all this, or have already arrived at my goal, but I press on to take hold of that for which Christ Jesus took hold of me. Brothers and sisters, I do not consider myself yet to have taken hold of it. But one thing I do: Forgetting what is behind and straining toward what is ahead, I press on toward the goal to win the prize for which God has called me heavenward in Christ Jesus.

PHIL 3:12-14

Are you familiar with Magnolia trees?

They require quite a bit of care and there was one just behind my house growing up. My dad taught me the best way to fertilize them so he wouldn't have to do all the work himself. Great, just what a teenage boy wants to learn!

Healthy Magnolias are known for producing countless flowers and they are truly majestic in full bloom. But their glory comes at a cost; they require lots of nutrients to sustain their beauty.

Timely and deep fertilization is the key to maintaining a Magnolia's health. Unfortunately, sprinkling the needed fertilizer on the ground around the tree does not work. The grass or ground cover under the tree loves it, but very little if any nutrients ever gets to the roots. Some people use slender fertilizer stakes that you nail into the top soil and they are an improvement, but much less than ideal.

The best fertilization strategy for a Magnolia is to use a specialized tool that delivers the fertilizer directly to the roots via water. Specifically, the pelletized nutrients are placed in a small plastic container that is connected to a water source as well as a thirty-inch, hollow steel rod. One end of the rod is screwed into the container while the other narrows to a point that includes several holes. The process is not complicated: Place the measured fertilizer into the container, connect it to a water hose, shove the rod into the ground two-to-four feet from the Magnolia's trunk and turn on the water. Wait until the fertilizer is gone and repeat this process all around the tree.

Was it hard work? Yes indeed!

And so is driving affirmed equipping values into a community's culture. It's an ongoing process that requires spiritual endurance and lots of effort. And it's not about hours, days, weeks or months; like a Magnolia, it takes years for a Jesus culture to exhibit majestic beauty.

Discipline and persistence is the price of equipping like Jesus

Catalyzing the Values of Equipping Like Jesus

In Chapter Five, I utilized Jethro's training model – pray, teach and show – as a way to capture how Jesus catalyzed His relational priorities among His disciples. Jesus' masterful skill and strategies become self-evident over time as a group of humble learners become world-changing value carriers of love. I call this process *"heart discipleship"*; helping receptive people encounter God, welcome His gracious love and then give it away to others. As I have already highlighted, this focus of Jesus was all about character formation and prepared His followers for a second stage of learning.

Through prayer, teaching and modeling, Jesus also catalyzed His equipping values within this same group. *"It was (Christ) himself who gave some apostles, the prophets, the evangelists, the pastors and teachers, to equip His people for works of service, so that the body of Christ may be built up"* (Eph 4:11-12). This process of training and preparing disciples to serve the needs of others is what I call *"ministry discipleship"*; helping receptive disciples discover their spiritual gifting and calling so they can effectively minister to others. This focus is all about capacity, and together with character, positions disciples for anointed service.

Instead of recounting how Jesus trained His twelve for ministry, however, I am going to use Jethro's template to provide an overview of my own journey. What follows is how I have sought to emulate His ways and drive Jesus' equipping values into my Peter, James, John and beyond. I am still a work in progress, but am trusting you will glean helpful insights from my life's focus.

Buckle Your Belt and Pray

Therefore put on the full armor of God, so that when the day of evil comes, you may be able to stand your ground, and after you have done everything, to stand. Stand firm then, with the belt of truth buckled around your waist...   *Eph 6:13-14*

Paul's renown passage on the armor of God in Ephesians 6 strikes me as directly related to all that he has been saying beforehand and it is a crystal-clear warning. He knows it is a battle to make Jesus the cornerstone. He knows it is a challenge to preach His Gospel to an audience that worships themselves and inanimate gods. He fully appreciates how hard it is for a Jesus house to reject worldly values and embrace Kingdom culture: selfless love and equipping-based empowerment. He also knows that endurance is a very real issue.

And so, this Apostle's concluding message to the church in Ephesus plus nearby communities is clear: Enduring faithfulness is a spiritual battle that demands that we be proactive (checkout Paul's goodbye to the Ephesian elders in Acts 20:28-30). I see this initially in Paul's "belt of truth" imagery. Given the military clothing of Paul's day, a belt was a crucial first step in preparing for a battle. This belt would gather any loose clothing so that a fighter's arms and legs were unhindered.[1] As we keep reading, Paul provides another related insight: Prayer is also a key strategy that accelerates our readiness for battle.

> *And pray in the Spirit on all occasions with all kinds of prayers and requests. With this in mind, be alert and always keep on praying for all the Lord's people.*　　　　*Eph 6:18*

In like fashion, I have sought to be a proactive intercessor when introducing and driving a culture of equipping-based empowerment. For decades, I have risen early every morning for time with Jesus and as it relates to my ministry, here are the kinds of reoccurring themes that I have voiced in the Throne Room:

My own needs and battles: Jesus asked His Father for help and as a house leader, I have done so as well! Truth be told, my ego and pride has consistently been a hindrance to my leadership effectiveness. Daily time with Jesus in order to worship Him, confess sin and receive His truth and strength has been and remains an absolute non-negotiable for my leadership within His house. Far and away, it has been the most important ingredient in sustaining my capacity to drive Kingdom culture and effectively serve and resource other leaders.[2] *Lord, help me to see the spec in my own eye and receive your grace!*

---

[1]　Walter L. Liefeld, *Ephesians (Downers Grove: IV Press, 1997), 163.*

[2]　It can be a challenge to keep track of all the people that need and depend upon your prayers. I have found index cards is a simple and dynamic way to ensure that I do not forget those I need to hold up.

The enemy's lies: Jesus taught us that the father of all lies is never far away. That has certainly been true in my life and the Jesus houses I have been a part of. How ironic that the enemy uses you and me as couriers of ungodliness as John, Lynn and Sam observed and experienced firsthand. I have consistently prayed that God would expose the lies we believe to His light and empower us to stand firm against them. *Lord, help me see our unbelief!*

Unity: As Jesus understood and prayed so well (John 16), many things stand in the way of unity within His communities. It is so easy for our distinctive spiritual gifts, personalities, natural talents and experiences to narrow our perspective! When we impose our myopic perspective on others, it becomes an obstacle to the Father's Kingdom. Truth be told, equipping the saints is a team sport! *Lord, help us to honor Your grace and gifts within others!*

Leaders for the harvest: Jesus highlighted few specific prayer needs, but this was one of them (Mt 9:37). Sometimes, we have not because we ask not. *Lord, send us men and women with relevant potential and anointings*!

Transformation: The families of origin you and I grew up in always have strongholds that impact our capacity to equip like Jesus does. Accordingly, this has been a place of consistent intercession as I have warred for my ministry partners. And don't be naïve, communities have strongholds as well. *Lord, change us from the inside out!*

Mentors: Jesus shared an obvious truth about those who equip us: *"The student is not above the teacher, but everyone who is fully trained will be like their teacher"* (Lk 6:40). None of my teachers were perfect and so I have needed to be discerning. What is of God and what is not? How has this truth impacted you? *Lord, give us discernment as we learn to follow You!*

My Tribe: Whatever human entity (community, movement, denomination, seminary, association etc.) you are a part of is far from perfect! In what ways does your tribe's identity, values, philosophy and history work against Kingdom culture? The Reformation's tenet that I have been focusing on – the priesthood of all believers -- remains an elusive objective for almost all tribes after hundreds of years.[3] *Lord, helps us to exchange human paradigms for your plan!*

My spiritual leadership over the years has been far from perfect. There is no doubt that at times, I have lacked vigilance in these prayer themes as though the enemy was not actively targeting my community. Nothing could be further from the truth; the father of lies (Jn 8:44) has been relentless for centuries.

If I could reboot my ministry and start over based what I now know, I would most certainly spend more time interceding for my colleagues with these kinds of prayers.

Intercession is the first step of implementation

Provide Practicals as You Teach

When I teach the five equipping values (Chapter Six), my audience consistently appreciates the simplicity of these priorities and their related slogans. It is usually not hard for them to understand and most can connect them to their own life experience.

But this paradigm, by itself, does not satisfy most of them. I have found that ministry leaders also want the practicals and ask questions like: *How do we walk-out these values on a day-to-day basis? What does it look like when these values have been fully implemented?*

The diagram below summarizes the five values I detail and has been very helpful in training leaders. As I unpack each value,

---

[3] Greg Ogden's book Unfinished Business: Returning the Ministry to the People of God (Harper Collins Publishing, 2003) is a must read.

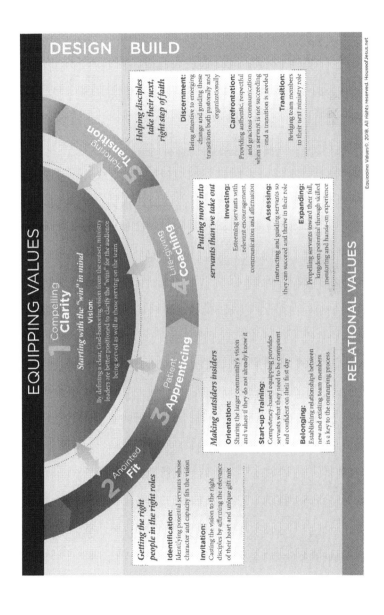

EQUIPPING VALUES

DESIGN

1 Compelling Clarity

Starting with the "win" in mind.

Vision:
By defining a clear, God-honoring vision from the outset, ministry leaders are better positioned to clarify the "wins" for the audience being served as well as those serving on the team.

2 Anointed Fit

Getting the right people in the right roles.

Identification:
Identifying potential servants whose character and capacity fits the vision

Invitation:
Casting the vision to the right disciples by affirming the relevance of their heart and unique gift mix

3 Patient Apprenticing

Making outsiders insiders.

Orientation:
Sharing the larger community's vision and values if they do not already know it

Start-up Training:
Competency-based equipping provides servants what they need to be competent and confident on their first day

Belonging:
Establishing relationships between new and existing team members is a key to the onramping process

BUILD

4 Life-Giving Coaching

Putting more into servants than we take out.

Investing:
Esteeming servants with relevant encouragement, communication and affirmation

Assessing:
Instructing and guiding servants so they can succeed and thrive in their role

Expanding:
Propelling servants toward their full, kingdom potential through skilled mentoring and hands-on experience

5 Honoring Transition

Helping disciples take their next, right step of faith.

Discernment:
Being attentive to emerging change and guiding these transitions both pastorally and organizationally

Carefrontation:
Providing authentic, respectful and gracious communication when a servant is not succeeding and a transition is needed

Transition:
Bridging team members to their next ministry role

RELATIONAL VALUES

I review the key driver(s), the types of related steps equippers will need to take and the reoccurring questions that leaders benefit from asking and answering.

An introductory teaching summary for this equipping diagram is included with the resources after this chapter and can be found on page 171. To be sure you understand my teaching terms, here are a few definitions:

Values: These are the five (5) equipping values modeled by the Father and Jesus as described by various passages in God's Word.

Key Drivers: These twelve (12) drivers are *process strategies* that accelerate the implementation of the five values. All are grounded in my twenty-plus years of experience and also detailed in Cousins' and Bugbee's Experiencing Leadershift application guide.

Related Steps: Each driver is accomplished as team equippers utilize their combined gifts and skills to complete a series of related action steps as needed; think of these as best practices.

Questions: One of my primary teaching strategies has been to help new and established equippers learn to ask and answer the right questions each step of the way. As you will see, a sampling of questions is included for each driver.

Redundant teaching enables equipping to become an established process

As already highlighted, additional resources on all these equipping values and related subjects can be found at **HouseofJesus.net.** It exists to provide ongoing, supplemental help for those who want to learn more.

Walk the Equipping Talk

As we have already learned, modeling was the third phase of Jethro's suggested training strategy. So, just to be clear, let me state a related and obvious truth: *Apart from Jesus, no Eph 4:11 leader equips servants perfectly; none.*

I wish I could say that after decades of effort I had mastered equipping and could model it perfectly, but that is simply not the case. I am better at walking out several of the five values than the others and the same can be said of the twelve key drivers. After twenty years, I am strong in some, seasoned in others and struggle with a few. So, here is another significant truth that I am repeating:

Walking out the equipping values is a "team sport"

As highlighted in the prior chapter, Jesus "gave" an APEST team (some call the gifts of Eph 4:11 a "fivefold team") the primary responsibility for equipping a community's disciples. So as one with a primary gift of teaching, I need to partner in this value-based training process with others, namely apostles, prophets, evangelists and pastors. Together, our combined voices can foster holistic ministry better than any of us can on our own. However, I am not suggesting that every ministry group needs all five kinds of APEST gifts present within its leadership. I am saying that groups greatly benefit when: 1) The point person(s) is affirmed as a disciple who has godly character and one of the Eph 4:11 gifts; 2) That this gifting is directly related to the group's vision and desired outcomes; 3) As needed, the influence of the other four giftings is present within the larger community and help shape the group's ministry and; 4) All the community's APEST equippers own and walk out the same philosophy of equipping.

Contemporary Perspectives on APEST: This fivefold theme is an important and expansive theme, but beyond the scope of this book. So, let me direct you to three current resources and one metaphor that has been very helpful to me. The three books as detailed in the bibliography are: *Primal Fire* (Cole); *Permanent Revolution* (Hirsch and Catchim) and *Creating a Missional Culture* (Woodward). Each seeks to explain the focus of these five gifts and how they partner together.

I have found Cole's broad, brush-stroke metaphor for these five spiritual gifts particularly helpful. He divides them into two categories: 1) The "Foundation Layers: The Start and Go Team" (apostles and prophets) and; 2) The "Builders: The Stay and Grow Team" (evangelists, pastors and teachers). Based on my experience, there is a lot of truth in this language which I included in my equipping diagram.

There is no doubt that my fondest memories of ministry are when I have been a part of team where foundation and building specialists honored each other's gifts, walked out a shared equipping philosophy, functioned in balance with one another and played to one another's strengths.

Having laid a foundation through prayer and teaching, here are the primary ways by which I have sought to constantly model and catalyze Jesus' equipping ways within my community.

Constantly Keeping God's Word Front and Center: The Bible has power (Heb 4:12) and as I have driven Jesus' values, I've repeatedly verbalized what it says and detailed how they relate to my equipping of others. The five equipping values are not sourced in Charlie, but Christ! In like fashion, I have memorized many of the passages I have quoted in this section and expected my key leaders to do the same. As Billy Graham attested, the phrase *"the Bible says"* followed by God's truth is transformational.

Constantly Look in the Mirror: To faithfully walk out the equipping values, leaders have to keep learning and growing.

Once again, *"Speed of the leader; speed of the team"* makes this very point. My teammates never expected me to be perfect, but they knew I was looking at my own flaws and striving to be better. I'm confident they saw that I had been practicing Jesus' ways for years.

Constantly Drive the Language: The power of a common language among all ministry leaders within a Jesus house is hard to overstate. It accelerates life-giving unity and collaboration. It accelerates leader development and effectiveness. It accelerates reproduction and transferability. It accelerates ministry expansion and Kingdom impact. Jesus' parables prove He understood this principle.

Constantly Involve the "Three": From observing Jesus, I have always known that my capacity for making a Kingdom difference was directly related to the breadth and depth of the equipping leaders I was developing. In other words, the challenge of ministry is seldom related to finding participants; it's finding and growing leaders. To that end, I have always zeroed in on my "Peter, James and John" disciples within my orbit and deeply invested in them.

Constantly Align Leadership Expectations to the Values: Those who have served under me know the drill: I expected myself and them to walk out the relational and equipping values. And as you know by now, I was motivated to codify these ideals so I could equip them better and clarify my expectations. This old adage about accountability is true: *"What gets measured gets managed."*

Constantly Link Equipping to Relationships: In my jargon, relational values and equipping values combine together to form ministry values. As a result, when I have trained disciples in equipping, it always comes back to the primacy of loving relationships. It's no longer a surprise for me to find a NT passage where both spiritual gifts and spiritual fruit are linked together. Check out 1 Pt 4:8-10 for a great example.

Constantly Affirm Alignment: When I see people exhibiting Jesus' ministry values, I let them know it as soon as possible. We all benefit from a genuine "Well done, good and faithful servant" affirmation!

Constantly Communicate with the "Seventy": Once I established equipping values and core leaders started to emerge, I sought to build an Eph 4 leadership community. And Jesus, in His infinite wisdom understood and modeled this strategy. We can see His fingerprints in the "seventy" highlighted in Luke 10. We can see an even larger leadership community coming together in Acts 1. Bottom-line: He formed a community of passionate followers, embedded the kingdom DNA in their souls and spirits, paved the way for the indwelling power of God, and then got out of their way. The result: a community of vested disciples who embraced His cornerstone message and values, and then replicated His model of disciple-making ministry to the "ends of the earth." Sounds like a good plan to me!

Constantly Look for Emerging Equippers: The better someone knows the equipping values and best practices, the more likely it is that they will be able to spot disciples with Eph 4:11 potential. Consequently, I have progressively become more effective at seeing the next generation of leaders with growing character and capacity. Once spotted, they are added to my intercession list, invited to my next teaching overview and woven into my apprenticing orbit. I could give you lots of names!

Modeling Jesus' equipping ways is a constantly unfolding process

Magnolia-Inspired Alignment

Leith Anderson knows more about the repetitive process needed to fertilize Magnolia trees than he probably realizes. Let me explain.

Leith is a well-respected and seasoned pastor who has written multiple books about accelerating the Kingdom. I respect him a great deal and years ago, his equipping testimony made a huge impression on me. I listened intently as he described his Jesus-like strategy that, from his perspective, was the most impactful leadership development process he had ever utilized.

In order to more strongly align his congregation to Jesus' values and mission, he got the idea to invite 6-8 leaders at a time to learn, discuss, and explore with him what being a kingdom-focused Jesus house means. In advance, the participants would read several relevant books and then meet together with him for six consecutive weeks. Concurrently, each would also visit and complete an assessment of another nearby Jesus house—a means to have these leaders look at a community's culture from an outsider's perspective.

After completing this regimen, these disciples better under-stood their own community's cornerstone, were fully grounded in its kingdom themes, had a more personal relationship with Leith, and exhibited more attentiveness to the principles of faithful living. At the time that I heard him, he had replicated this discipline eight (8) times a year for six (6) years. His conclusion (and mine): This repetitive process was highly catalytic at aligning the community's leadership to its Christ-centered cornerstone.

Relentlessly aligning godly equippers to His message and ways is what the Master did

Aligning a Culture to Equipping

Discipline and persistence is the price of equipping like Jesus

Intercession is the first step of implementation

Redundant teaching enables equipping to become an established process

Walking out the equipping values is a "team sport"

Modeling Jesus' equipping ways is a constantly unfolding process

Relentlessly aligning godly equippers to His message and ways is what the Master did

90°

Section Two: Equipping Values Statement

Source: Antioch New England

Equipping Values

Jesus was a true servant leader who modeled equipping-based empowerment from a heart of humility and submission. As His servants, we collectively affirm His ways and our complete devotion to them.

Compelling Clarity
Starting with the win in mind

Our Father is never confused about His preferred future, nor the process to achieve it. We follow His lead in every situation by first affirming the desired outcomes—for both the ministry's target audience and those serving. *See also Ps. 33:11; Is. 46:10-11; Jer. 29:11; Acts 1:8; Eph. 1:11, 2:10, 3:10-11; Rev. 7, 21*

Anointed Fit
Getting the right people in the right roles

God chose Moses because he was a man of proven character and capacity. He was just the right person for God's plan: delivering Israel out of Egypt and to the Promised Land. Team leaders follow God's pattern by utilizing fruitfulness (character) and spiritual gifting (capacity) as their primary filters to identify needed team members. Entrusting ministry into the right, faithful hands sets the stage for Kingdom success. *See also Ex. 18:13-27; Ps. 78:72; Eph. 4:16; 2 Tim. 2:2; 1 Pt. 4:10*

Patient Apprenticing
Setting others up for success

Our God always knows what we need to get started well. The Father knew what Abram needed to take his first steps of faith. Jesus knew what Saul needed to embrace his new calling to be the Apostle Paul. Indeed, all God's followers are His workmanship, and He equips us to step into the good works that He has prepared for us. In like fashion, we help those serving with what they need to be confident and competent, ready to step into their new roles and make a Kingdom difference. *See also Gen. 12-15; Acts 6:1-7, Early discipleship of Paul (Acts 9-13; Gal. 1-2); Eph. 2:10; 2 Tim. 2:2*

Life-Giving Coaching
Putting more in than we take out

Jesus purposely lived His life in full view of His disciples. He embedded the Father's values in them while He ate, slept, taught, healed, and revealed the Kingdom of God in their midst. As this process unfolded, He increasingly released them to minister in His name. In Jesus' final hours, He promised the Spirit of Truth to continue their instruction and guide them in the Father's worldwide vision. Ministry leaders are similarly called to partner with the Spirit as they model, observe, sustain, and release those serving to run their ministry race with endurance and hear their Father's "well done!" *See also Mt. 25:14-30; Jesus and His disciples (Jn. 14-16); Eph. 4:11-12; Paul's apprenticing of Timothy and many others*

Honoring Transitions
Helping people take their next steps of faith

Our God always guides His children through times of change. After His resurrection, Jesus walked with His followers to get them ready for His ascension and the Spirit's arrival. Jesus also graciously restored Peter after the pain and humiliation of three denials. He calls us to reflect the compassionate heart of God by honoring the ministry transitions of those around us. These transitions occur for many reasons: at times, a change of life seasons or increased capacity prompts a new focus. At other times, ministry transitions stem from a lack of character, capacity, or fit. Whatever the reasons, Jesus' example of honor and honesty guides how we care for those who serve Him. *See also Elijah passing his mantle to Elisha (1 Kgs. 19:19); Eph. 4:15; Jesus readies his followers for His departure (Jn. 14-21; Acts 1); Paul honors the Ephesian elders as he departs (Acts 20:13-38)*

Section Two:
Equipping Case Study

Equipping on the Fly
An Interview with Samuel Zwingli and John Prickett

These dear brothers are a part of a church planting movement that has 30+ churches in the US and even more teams serving around the world. In the summer of 2016, they and 2,000 other servants from these US congregations ministered in Europe under the banner "Engage the Crisis." This initiative had three primary goals: meet the needs of the region's new Middle Eastern refugees, share and exemplify a message of grace in order to make disciples and mobilize North American disciples to serve.

Samuel was asked to lead one of the ten ministry bases in Europe and was honored by the opportunity. At the same time, the invitation was somewhat overwhelming. He had never been in charge of something quite like this, plus there were only a handful of months to get ready and his base's staff would include people he had never met. One of his first moves was to ask his friend John to co-lead with him in the start-up and launch phase.

What follows is an interview with both after they returned and had had time to process their experience.

Charlie: Samuel, in the midst of very challenging circumstances, the consistent testimony of your base's leaders is that the team thrived and operated at a very high level of trust and effectiveness. How do you explain their experience?

Samuel: *In retrospect, I can now see that our leadership team's success hinged on several factors. First, a shared leadership approach with my partner John proved to be very fruitful. My apostolic bent was tempered by his pastoral personality and gift mix. One plus one equaled three – what an important lesson learned. Second, John and I benefitted immeasurably from already having a common language for ministry faithfulness even though we had never worked together. From day one, we shared your paradigm of equipping and it unified our partnership as we sought to accomplish this audacious vision. Third, there were others on our leadership team that had also been schooled in these same ministry values and even those that had not, picked up on it pretty quickly. As a result, our leadership team served well together and were on the same page from day one.*

Charlie: John, what did you see from your perspective? How did you guys figure out how to share the point person role?

John: *We were just talking about that. Samuel and I had a pivotal conversation several months before everybody hit the ground. We were talking about how we were going to co-lead together. That's part of this story as well; how do you co-lead a team and not just have a solo leader? How does that work? So in that conversation we were discussing how are we going to do this. I explained to Samuel my understanding of the equipping values that you and I had been talking about. I remember voicing my desire to make this paradigm the foundation of how we lead our base. I was thrilled when he jumped onboard one-hundred percent. We agreed that we would make the equipping values our common decision rules for everything we did and use this language throughout our leadership team.*

Charlie: So, tell me about the start-up of your leadership team. What did that look like?

John: *It all happened so fast! I actually don't remember huddling everybody together and hashing out our leadership DNA although that might have been valuable. The projects didn't lend itself to that. In reality, we did a lot of orientation and coaching on the fly as real time situations came up. Some of the leaders had a baseline understanding of these equipping values, but no more than half. We also ended up coming up with three missional values which also accelerated our effectiveness.*

Charlie: Sounds like the challenges of every day ministry became a great excuse to train and invest in your staff.

John: *Exactly! Some people wanted Samuel and I to make all the decisions and we put the ownership of the ministry right back in their lap. As you say, we used ministry to equip people rather than using people to accomplish ministry.*

Samuel: *It's not like we knew everything; we just had more experience than most. We were frequently as clueless as they were so we kept bringing them back to our missional and equipping values.*

It was that way all summer. We constantly had new teams of servants arriving and all new problems. People would come to us with all kinds of questions and we would point them to our values and invite discussion. Since we value such and such, what do you think we should do? And then we'd have a little coaching moment, share a couple of ideas and then ask them for their best solution. If it didn't feel like the right answer, we just kept the process going. We didn't always come up with perfect answers, but our actions always satisfied our values. And really, that is all we really had time for.

Charlie: If you had never encountered the equipping values, do you think you would have been more like Moses before Jethro and try to provide people with the right answers as opposed to helping them make the decisions themselves?

John: *I think so. These equipping values prioritize empowering others as the training process unfolds. Obviously, it's part and parcel to apprenticing people and then coaching them.*

Samuel: *I agree with John. Without a values-based approach upfront, we would've tried to manage the chaos by having our fingers into every pie.*

Charlie: How about a few stories of people who responded particularly well to being empowered to be value-based leaders?

Samuel: *John, your wife Jessie is a great example.*

Charlie, she had been a part of some of the trainings that you had done and was able to take her assignment and run with it. She provided oversight for what we called "engagement ministry"; it was compassion care for refugees.

She instantly understood her running lanes, how to make challenging decisions and figure out complex situations all in the midst of one of the greatest humanitarian crises in recent history.

John: *Another good example was Audrey.*

The suggested team design included an administrative position to assist the base leaders. From the start, however, we only wanted to have a person who was confident of making administrative decisions without constantly asking for confirmation.

Audrey had come with rave reviews from her home church, but we didn't have any grid for understanding either her gifting or capacity. So, we created a short-term role so we could see if it was going to be a good fit for her and us.

In short order, she demonstrated herself to be really competent so we apprenticed her in the missional and equipping values. We talked about them and gave her examples. This training gave her a clear mental map and within a week, she was making $10,000 decisions.

Charlie: How did your German national partners respond to your value-based leadership strategy?

John: *I remember being in a meeting with one of our partners and we were using your jargon. He's been in ministry for a long time and was impressed by the way we were operating. At one point, he just stopped our discussion, and affirmed our values and the way we were allowing them to define our team process. He really noticed how they fostered unity and empowered people. He wanted to learn more!*

Charlie: By the end of the summer, what were some of your leadership team's takeaways?

John: *One stands out for me: If you're going to do ministry Jesus' way, it will require flipping a common notion on its head. It is so common for ministry leaders to spend the bulk of their time trying to multiply fishes and loaves for the 5,000, rather than equipping their core "apostles" to make it happen. And when this happens, leaders frequently get neglected for the sake of the masses. Looks to me like Jesus, however, invested in the 12 and then the 70 in order to reach the masses. The end game of reaching the whole earth with the Gospel and disciples being native to every people group is still the same, but Jesus' process seems to be counter-cultural these days.*

I think we did this as well as we could. The human needs were so enormous it became a battle every day. There were thousands upon thousands of refugees and we all had a nagging question: Are we doing enough? In the end, we fought for and achieved some measure of balance between the needs of the team's servants and the refugees our team was called to serve.

Samuel: *Another that came out of our debriefing time was that a shared leadership model can work. I actually co-led with two people over the course of the summer. John partnered with me the first half of the summer and then Phil jumped in mid-stream.*

One key to our partnership came up as John and I debriefed about this recently, namely humility. There were a couple of defining moments where it became pretty intense. Not to toot our own horn, but our intense humility enabled the sum of our parts to be greater than either of us. It was a rare and really special victory because in theory, that should not have worked according to certain assumptions in our ministry world. But I think it did work. It was really powerful because we brought such different things to the table and in humility, our service was beautiful. I think that was a big one.

John: *One related thought. I think it's important to clarify that not everyone understood the values and how they were sourced in Jesus. There were certain types of people that just did not understand our approach and we did not have time to apprentice them in the way that they needed. They needed much more clarity to be set up for success. The pace was so fast and the expectation of how much was going to be accomplished in such a short period of time was so great. This was a point of tension: trying to walk out these values that advocate for excellence while at the same time, addressing a crisis situation. It was really difficult.*

Samuel: *Sorry, there is one more insight from our debrief; this experience really confirmed the value of anointed fit. People had arrived with some knowledge of the roles that would be available and had their own preconceived expectations of what they thought would be cool to do. But we placed people strictly based on their gifting. In the end, any number of people commented about how their role was not what they had picked, but it ended up be a lifegiving place to serve; that was encouraging to hear.*

Charlie: I can't help but notice the duality of your team's success: lots of refugees were well served, but so were your teammates.

John: *When I returned from serving, I wrestled with whether or not we had even been successful. We did not achieve some of the lofty goals we established as it relates to the refugees and what would specifically result from our outreach.*

At the end of the day, I came back to success being faithful living according to Jesus' values and then it's up to the Holy Spirit. We loved each other well. We acted in humility. There were people on our base who were apprenticed, empowered, coached, believed in. So I felt like I could walk away with a good conscience.

Samuel: *When I have thought about this issue in the year since, one of the things I think about most is a particular intern named Jeff. As I recall, he had not been invited into any role of influence in his home church.*

But on our base, we only had 50 staff and he was one of them. We discerned he had a strong prophetic voice and we empowered this gifting. He was one of the primary prophetic voices for that entire summer, but he was just a college sophomore. We'd walk into meetings and look at him and say, what's the word of the Lord? Not exactly in those terms, but that experience changed his life.

John: *He was not your typical leader. He was soft-spoken, more introverted, reserved, but major integrity, reliable, faithful, honest, genuine.*

Samuel: *So, as I reflect on that crazy summer, some of the greatest things that came out of the equipping paradigm were a couple of people who are trained and empowered for the first time in their lives and marked forever. Someone gave them authority commensurate with the character that they possessed and a role that suited them.*

Charlie: Guys, thanks for sharing your story!

Section Two:
Equipping Culture Survey

Walking out Jesus' culture of equipping is realized through an ongoing process of realignment to His values and ways. Accordingly, He calls us into a transformational process: *"If anyone would come after me, let them deny themselves, pick up their cross and follow Me" (Mk 8:35).*

With this in mind, identifying the gaps between Jesus' values and our reality through focused feedback is valuable. When specific areas of growth are clarified, disciples will be able to more clearly see related strongholds and identify the relevant truths and strategies that will accelerate godliness.

What follows is an example of an assessment tool—an equipping culture survey. It is based on the equipping values and process strategies highlighted in Chapter Six and Eight, and can be used to assess a person, a team and/or a whole community. If your community has already established and affirmed its own equipping ideals, simply adapt this template to fit your language.

Equipping Culture Survey Template

Instructions: This instrument is designed to be a **confidential exercise** that assesses the leadership behavior of a predetermined "subject"—a person, team or larger community.

In this survey, there are two exercises for each of the five (5) equipping values. The first utilizes a continuum of leadership style with opposing preferences on each end. Those completing the assessment are asked to circle the word that best captures how they typically see the "subject".

#1 LEADERSHIP PREFERENCES	HIGH	MODERATE	LOW	BALANCE	LOW	MODERATE	HIGH	#2 LEADERSHIP PREFERENCES

Example: Look at the two leadership preferences listed under *Clarity* – Perfectionism and Urgency. They are mutually exclusive behaviors and both work against the value of Clarity as I have defined it. Which of these two bests describes the "subject" of this assessment? Now circle one of the three qualifiers (low, moderate or high) to describe the strength of that preference. If you see the subject exhibiting both behaviors equally, circle "balanced".

The second part asks assessors to rank three equipping behaviors listed for each value. The strongest and most visible behavior should be ranked with a "1" and the weakest with a "3".

Special Note: If the "subject" is more than one person – i. e. *"members of the leadership team"*—answers should reflect the entire group being assessed. Evaluators should trust their gut and respond with their first impressions.

Value #1: Compelling Clarity....
Starting with the "win" in mind

Definition: Ministry leaders define a clear, God-honoring vision from the outset that includes: 1) The "wins" for the audience being served and 2) The desired outcomes for the servants that will be needed to realize the vision.

In regards to *Clarity,* circle the word that best describes the subject's leadership style.

PERFECTIONISM leads to getting stuck on detailing clarity resulting in demotivated teammates	HIGH	MODERATE	LOW	BALANCE	LOW	MODERATE	HIGH	URGENCY leads to launching without clarity often resulting in team confusion and disappointment

Rank the following *Clarity* behaviors (1-3) with #1 being the strongest:

_____ Leads with clarity about the vision: what it will look like when its been achieved

_____ Understands and easily articulates the desired outcomes for the target audience

_____ Leads from a place of clarity about what success looks like for team servants

The *Equipping Culture Survey* in its entirety is now available at HouseofJesus.net

Section Two: Teaching Summary

Introduction to Equipping

Value #1: Compelling Clarity...
Starting with the "win" in mind

Is 14:24; 46:10-11; Ps 33:11; Eph 3:10-11; Jer 29:11; Eph 1:11; Rev 7:9ff; 21.

Driver

Vision

As God models, it is best to see the end from the beginning. By defining a clear, God-honoring vision from the outset, ministry leaders are better positioned to clarify: 1) The "wins" for the audience being served and 2) The kinds of servants that will be needed to realize the vision and what success will look like for them.

Related Steps:

1. Begin the process of defining the *time-sensitive vision* that leaders are discerning for the next year(s). (A *timeless vision* is one that will never be fully realized and typically serves as a consistent slogan for a team or community such as "*Love God; Love One Another; Love the Lost*".) As needed, also articulate and affirm the vision's related theology, philosophic assumptions, mission etc.

2. Detail the *desired outcomes* or "wins" for both the target audience of the vision and the servants who will serve within the ministry.

3. Sustain the process of clarity by empowering diverse teams to collaboratively shape the vision's planning process by specifying the needed phases, mile markers, timelines, teams, resources, strategies and objectives. <u>Clarify no more or less than is needed</u>.

<u>Questions:</u>

- What will the community / ministry look like when the time-sensitive vision is realized? What does success look like? What will life be like when we get there?

- Based on the discerned vision, what are the "wins" for both the target audience of our ministry and the servants who are part of the team? What does success look like for each?

- What are the best strategies for achieving the desired outcomes we have discerned? How should these strategies be sequenced to maximize their impact? What is the scope, nature and dimensions of the team(s) that will be needed to be activate these strategies? What resources will be needed in order to accomplish these strategies?

The *Teaching Summary* in its entirety is now available at HouseofJesus.net

---

Final Thoughts

After John, Lynn and Sam went their separate ways, what would they have seen and experienced if they had found communities that were aligned to Jesus?

Communities without crippling strongholds imported from the surrounding world....

Where their cornerstone is never a personality or syncretic ideology;

Where Jesus' Gospel does not have to compete with legalism, humanism or idols;

Where relationships are not undermined by arrogance, prejudice or manipulation;

Where leaders don't abandon equipping for usery, control or personal gain.

Instead, communities that wholeheartedly[1] ....

Prioritize Jesus as the defining cornerstone to which everything is aligned;

Proclaim His Gospel of grace with their words and lives (Say);

Exemplify His selfless love within their relational sphere (Be);

Equip and empower disciples so they can fulfill their calling to God's mission (Do);

---

[1] This is a biblical theme that is worthy of your time and energy. Check out Rick and Diane Bewsher's book entitled *Wholehearted: Tending Your Heart through Being Discipled by Jesus* (Zulon Press). It's loaded with relevant pearls that will transform your life.

If John, Lynn and Sam had located a Jesus house marked by the convergence of these four foundational elements, they would have walked into the Upper Room and the days that followed (Acts 1:15ff):

A critical mass of equipped, Jesus-house catalysts...
> Vigilantly praying as they waited for God to speak and lead;
> Leaning into God's guidance and one another as new leaders are anointed;
> Responding to the Spirit's presence, power and movement;
> Proclaiming the Good News with conviction and joy;
> Standing their ground in the face of institutional criticism and abuse;
> Devoted to God's Word and listening for His voice;
> Committed to unity and the gathered community;
> Awed by God's power as He moves;
> Courageously giving to one another;
> Worshiping with passion and expectancy;
> Living in authentic community;
> Rejoicing in God's goodness;
> Walking the talk and talking the walk.

Simply put, a community of men and women incarnating the words and ways of Jesus; *a living testimony of God's grace fueled by selfless love and equipping-based empowerment.*

A Concluding Thought

I have not yet experienced a community that is fully aligned to Jesus and I'm not sure I will during my life on earth.

At the same time, I have tasted an Acts-like convergence of Jesus' words and ways within a community where His Spirit's power is on display.

Sometimes it happens in worship settings;
Sometimes it happens in the desperation of suffering;
Sometimes it happens in personal visits to the Throne Room;
Sometimes it happens by complete surprise;
Sometimes it happens when there is great expectancy;

But it regularly happens when I, and we, are fully aligned to Jesus.

So, as a long-time resident of His house, let me leave you with one additional reality I keep seeing and experiencing:

Jesus' Words and Ways fuels Kingdom Impact

Without question, Jesus' Gospel message by itself is impactful. His Good News is the perfect accelerant for spiritually awakening men's and women's hearts. It is the power of salvation for all who believe, affirm His Lordship and ask for forgiveness.

But to catalyze the Kingdom impact of Pentecost, a community will necessarily need additional accelerants beyond Jesus' Words. It will also need Jesus' Ways: a supernatural culture of loving relationships and equipping-based empowerment.

So here is my challenge: put Jesus' example and Paul's teaching to the test.

Make Jesus the cornerstone of your community and fully align it to what He said (a Gospel of grace), who He was (loving relationships) and what He did (equipping-based empowerment).

Let me know how it turned out at HouseofJesus.net.

All for Him!

Bibliography

Addison, Steve. *What Jesus Started*: Joining the Movement -- Changing the World. Downers Grove: InterVarsity Press, 2012.

Backlund, Steve. *The Culture of Empowerment*: How to Champion People. Igniting Hope Ministries, 2016.

Bandy, Thomas G. *Moving Off the Map*: A Field Guide to Changing the Congregation. Nashville: Abingdon, 1998.

Bewsher, Rick and Diane Bewsher. *Wholehearted:* Tending Your Heart through being Discipled by Jesus. Maitland: Zulon Press, 2018.

Bridges, William. *Managing Transitions*: Making the Most of Change. Cambridge: Da Capo Press, 2003.

Cladis, George. *Leading the Team Based Church*: How Pastors and Church Staffs can Grow Together into a Powerful Fellowship of Leaders. San Francisco: Jossey-Bass Leadership Network Series, 1999.

Cole, Neil. *Organic Church*: Growing Faith Where Life Happens. San Francisco: Jossey-Bass Leadership Network Series, 2005.

Cole, Neil. *Primal Fire*: Reigniting the Church with the Five Gifts of Jesus. Carol Stream: Tyndale House Publishing, 2014.

Cousins, Don, and Bruce Bugbee. *Experiencing Leadershift*: A Step-by-Step Strategy for Church and Ministry Leaders. Colorado Springs: David C Cook, 2010.

Cousins, Don. *Experiencing Leadershift*: Letting Go of Leadership Heresies. Colorado Springs: David C Cook, 2010.

Ferguson, Dave, and Jon Ferguson. *Exponential*: How You and Your Friends can Start a Missional Movement. Grand Rapids, Zondervan, 2010.

Gorman, Michael J. *Cruciformity*: Paul's Narrative Spirituality of the Cross. Grand Rapids: Wm. B Eerdmans Publishing, 2001.

Halley, Charles. *The Heart of the Matter*: Changing the World God's Way. Lake Hickory Resources, 2006.

Hirsch, Alan, and Tim Catchim. *The Permanent Revolution*: Apostolic Imagination and Practice for the 21st Century. San Francisco: Jossey-Bass Leadership Network Series, 2005.

Liefeld, Walter L. *Ephesians.* Downers Grove: InterVarsity Press, 1997.

Mancini, Will. *Church Unique*: How Missional Leaders Cast Vision, Capture Culture and Create Movement. San Francisco: Jossey-Bass Leadership Network Series, 2008.

Neese, Zach. *How to Worship a King*: Prepare Your Heart; Prepare Your World; Prepare the Way. Dallas: Gateway Create Publishing, 2012.

Nouwen, Henri J. M. *In the Name of Jesus*: Reflections on Jesus' Leadership. Freiburg: Crossroad Publishing Company, 1992.

Ogden, Greg. *Unfinished Business*: Returning the Ministry to the People of God. New York: Harper Collins Publishing, 2012.

Rinehart, Stacy. *Upside Down*: The Paradox of Servant Leadership. Colorado Springs: NavPress Publishing, 1998.

Rogers, Everett M. *Diffusion of Innovation.* New York: The Free Press, 1995.

Silk, Danny. *Culture of Honor*: Sustaining a Supernatural Environment. Shippensburg: Destiny Image Publishers Inc, 2009.

Thompson, James W. *The Church According to Paul*: Rediscovering the Community Conformed to Christ. Grand Rapids: Baker Academic, 2014.

Woodward, J. R. *Creating a Missional Culture*: Equipping the Church for the Sake of the World. Downers Grove: InterVarsity Press, 2012.

About the Author

As followers of Jesus, we want our community to feel and run like His house.

Charlie Halley has spent his adult life trying to wrap his mind and leadership habits around Jesus' culture of love and equipping.

The Kingdom culture insights he teaches and writes about aren't just theory. They've been honed through a decades long journey of discovery, confession, breakthrough and influence.

He has tasted the joy that comes when a group of people invites Jesus to transform their culture and structures, but he's also felt the pain of brokenness when these biblical strategies were ignored.

Rooted in God's Word, the values and methods Charlie discusses have been validated within the Jesus houses he has served either on staff or as a consultant and coach. He's also written an earlier book on these themes: *The Heart of the Matter: Changing the World's God's Way* and holds graduate degrees in theology and business.

Outside the Kingdom, he spent a season catalyzing culture in the marketplace. As president/general manager of a multimillion-dollar retail business, he revitalized a failing 60-yearold enterprise and established a value-based culture aligned to its new ownership.

Most importantly, Charlie has been married to his wife Mary Lou for 42 years, and they've raised three great sons in Charles, John, and Thomas.

To learn more about Charlie, you can visit **HouseofJesus.net**

First, thanks for reading **The House of Jesus**! I hope it helped you reflect on your own understanding and journey with Jesus.

I have two big questions for you, as we wrap things up. The first is...

1) Does Your Experience Resemble a Jesus House?

Did you identify with John, Lynn, or Sam in my fable?

Have you been searching for a Jesus house where the Master's message is fueled by His culture of selfless love and equipping-based empowerment?

Or do you have vision to transform your current culture so that it is more aligned to Jesus' ways?

If you've been searching for a process to accelerate Kingdom culture in your own setting, then my next question is this...

2) Want to Continue the Journey?

We are building a learning community among people who are committed to catalyzing Jesus-aligned cultures: *Being who He was and Doing what He did.*

Visit us at **HouseofJesus.net.** You'll find resources to help you transform your current culture, find available coaching and training to go deeper in these truths and meet like-minded believers.

Take the next step. I look forward to seeing you online!

Charlie

HouseofJesus.net

54051018R00098

Made in the USA
Columbia, SC
26 March 2019